# JAMES MARTIN'S
## SPANISH ADVENTURE

This book is dedicated to my old college lecturer Ken Allanson, who placed me on the right path from the start and set me on the journey to a career I still care about and love as much as I did when we first met 40 years ago. Thank you. I owe you more than you will ever know.

# JAMES MARTIN'S
## SPANISH ADVENTURE

### 80 FANTASTIC RECIPES *FROM* AROUND SPAIN

Photography by Dan Jones

QUADRILLE

# INTRODUCTION

I've travelled to some fabulous places in my time and eaten some incredible food and, as you will be aware from the previous TV series, it's been a joy to bring the best food and produce into your home. Now I'm so excited to visit a country whose cuisine I love but know very little about. Of all the trips I have wanted to take, this is the one I was most looking forward to... Don't get me wrong, the others have been a joy, but heading to a country you haven't visited much but have a passion for its ingredients fills you with excitement. Not knowing what you will find, discovering more about the food you know and love in its original setting, and learning more about where it comes from makes the experience so special.

This is a real voyage of discovery for me. I'm going to delve deep into the food offerings of the different regions, go off the beaten track to find hidden gems, as well as getting to grips with the classics that we all know and love. Spain is a country with amazing culinary diversity and it was my mission to experience it all. Well, as much as my six-week trip would allow! What I quickly discovered is how passionate the Spanish people are about local and regional food.

In this book, and TV series, I'll be getting underneath the skin of Spain, discovering the history and culture of the country's diverse regions through food. My adventure begins in San Sebastián in the north east of Spain. From there I travel to the agricultural region of La Rioja before hitting the northern coastline again,

visiting Bilbao and Asturias. Then it's across to Galicia in the north west, experiencing the furanchos, where the locals open their homes to serve wine from the vineyard in jugs, with no more than five tapas, for just 3 months of the year.

The UNESCO world heritage town of Santiago de Compostela and its cathedral end the famous El Camino de Santiago pilgrimage for some 400,000 people a year. There are some treats in store here. You have to visit María Jesus at her small bakery just round the back of the cathedral and taste the tarta de Santiago she makes by hand in her 100-year-old oven – it is truly special. At the fishing port of Vigo, the bread and octopus are a wonderful combination. Try Diego Martín's bread from his newly opened bakery in the city and enjoy the simply cooked octopus from La Aldeana with olive oil and salt, plus the prawns, which are just amazing.

I then journey inland to Castile and León, where I visit José Gordón at his remarkable restaurant Bodega El Capricho, serving the greatest beef I have ever tasted and will ever taste. What's depressing is that I won't taste anything as good until I visit him again! This is one place you must go and experience for yourself, and also enjoy a tour around the farm. Just wait until you see the size of the fences, even before you see the Barroso cattle weighing up to 1,700kg. Visiting José is one of the very best food experiences I've ever had. I can go on and on about how good this restaurant is, so just go, please.

From here, Spain's vibrant capital, Madrid, offers a vast array of bars and restaurants to choose from. A must is the fried squid that everyone seems to queue for, as are the churros at the Chocolatería San Ginés, which has been serving hordes of people since 1894. But, for me, the highlight here was meeting blind food critic Jonatan Armengol and his dog Calo, as they showed me around the markets and he cooked for me at his place. It's the very essence of what Spain is all about – people couldn't have been any more hospitable and helpful. Maybe it's the weather, as they do say in Madrid that the sun shines 300 days a year, and locals are nicknamed cats as they like to go out and party every night. If you do go out to party, you have to go to Casa Alberto. It's over 200 years old and is owned and run by Alfonso Delgado, who produces and serves Madrid's famous vermouth – just wait until you try it. The drink, the bar, the place and the company are all epic. The aged vermouth is really special, and as you sit at the bar on stools, chatting away and watching the world go by, I can think of little better.

Next up is Extremadura and Castilla-La Mancha, where the famous Manchego cheese comes from. Then it's on to the fabulous region of Andalusia, with stop-offs in Seville, Cádiz, Málaga, Córdoba and Granada. Then, as I continue along the south coast, I take in Murcia, the Costa Brava, the port city of Valencia, famed for its rice fields, and then on to Catalonia and the coastal metropolis of Barcelona. Finally, my adventure will come to a delicious end in Girona.

What a joy it was searching out key ingredients, sampling the fine dining, rustic eateries and traditional recipes that make Spain one of the most exciting countries in the world for gastronomy. And to top it all off, I visited the Roca brothers at their amazing 3-star restaurant and walked with them as they made their daily pilgrimage, with the entire staff, for lunch at their mother and father's small restaurant, 5 minutes' walk away.

I loved every minute and can't wait to go back, if only to experience once again the custom of people enjoying the amazing food they produce, much of which is the very best there is anywhere, without any pomp and circumstance. This book shows you a mere snippet of what to use and what to cook with the best ingredients I've had on any road trip I've done yet. Welcome to Spain – it's one hell of a place!

# LIGHT BITES

# LEEK AND LARDONS WITH A WARM HAZELNUT DRESSING

**Serves 4**

4 large leeks
200g lardons
25ml olive oil
100g hazelnuts
½ white onion, finely diced
small bunch of parsley, chopped
1 tablespoon Dijon mustard
2 tablespoons oyster sauce
2 tablespoons hazelnut oil
1 tablespoon sherry vinegar
juice of 1 lemon

**This Riojan recipe celebrates fabulous-tasting leeks, which are blackened on the BBQ and then mixed with a warm hazelnut dressing and lardons for a beautiful contrast in textures. Delicious as a light bite or as a side as part of a larger BBQ spread.**

Heat a BBQ until hot and the coals are white.

Place the leeks directly onto the hot coals and cook for 8 minutes until charred all over, turning halfway through.

Fry the lardons in the oil for 5–6 minutes until crisp. Drain the fat into a large bowl, pop the lardons onto a tray, then toast the hazelnuts in the same pan.

Mix the onion, parsley, mustard, oyster sauce, hazelnut oil, vinegar and lemon juice with the lardon fat, finishing with the toasted hazelnuts.

Remove the charred outer leaves of the leeks, then slice and pop onto a platter. Sprinkle over the lardons and spoon over the hazelnut dressing to serve.

# CHORIZO AND WHITE BEAN SOUP

**Serves 4**

---

200g dried alubias blancas
    (white beans)
100ml olive oil
4 garlic cloves, chopped
1 onion, diced
pinch of pimentón ahumado
    (smoked paprika)
100g chorizo picante, diced
400ml chicken stock
1 teaspoon sea salt
8 slices of Ibérico ham, to serve

### For the picada
2 slices of baguette, cubed
25ml olive oil
1 garlic clove
pinch of salt
50g almonds, toasted
a few leaves of flat-leaf parsley

**Some of Spain's finest produce combined in a simple soup. Alubias blancas is Spanish for 'white beans', which are cooked with a spicy chorizo and then finished off with slices of Ibérico ham. Picada is a paste of fried bread, nuts, garlic, olive oil and herbs typically used in Catalan cuisine to thicken and flavour dishes such as soups and stews.**

Soak the beans overnight in plenty of water, then drain. Pop into a pan, cover with water and bring to the boil. Reduce the heat and simmer for 1 hour until the beans are just soft. Drain and set aside.

To make the picada, fry the bread cubes in the oil until crisp. Meanwhile, pound the garlic and salt in a pestle and mortar, then add the almonds and pound together. Add the fried bread and parsley and pound until it resembles a thick paste.

For the soup, add half the oil to a deep pan and gently fry the garlic, onion, pimentón and chorizo for 3–4 minutes until softened. Then add the remaining oil, the cooked beans and stock and bring to the boil. Reduce the heat and gently simmer for 5 minutes. Season with the salt and gently mix in the picada.

To serve, ladle the soup into bowls and top with slices of Ibérico ham.

# ASTURIAS STEAK AND CHEESE SANDWICH

**Serves 2**

---

1 cucumber

300g sirloin steak

15cm centre cut of a thick bloomer loaf

olive oil, for drizzling

150g Manchego cheese, grated

2 x 50g slices of Tetilla cheese

2 tablespoons red pepper mayonnaise

1 little gem lettuce, leaves separated

1 tomato, sliced

1 large pickled onion, sliced

sea salt

**This recipe uses not one but two types of cheese, and it is a corker. The cheese is just the crowning glory, as this sandwich begins with a generous dollop of red pepper mayonnaise on the base layer of bread. Followed by lettuce, tomatoes, then comes the succulent steak, some melted soft cheese, pickles, slices of my barbecued cucumber and the cheesy crown of bread on top. However you decide to tuck in, this is one epic sandwich.**

Heat a BBQ until hot and the coals are white.

Place the cucumber directly onto the coals, cook for 3–4 minutes, then set aside to cool.

Generously salt the steak, pop onto the BBQ rack and cook for 3–4 minutes. Flip over and repeat. Remove from the BBQ and leave to rest for 5 minutes, then slice.

Slice the bread in half horizontally. Drizzle with a little olive oil and char on both sides on the BBQ.

Remove the BBQ grill rack and place a cast-iron tray onto the BBQ. When hot, add the Manchego to the tray, then sit the top of the bread on top. When golden and crispy, take off the heat and curl the cheese up to from cheesy crisps.

Heat the slices of Tetilla cheese gently until hot, bubbling and stringy. On the bottom half of the bread, spoon the mayo all over, then add the lettuce, tomato, sliced steak, Tetilla cheese and pickled onion. Finish with the sliced cucumber and sit the cheesy bread lid on top.

# LA RIOJA TAPAS TWO WAYS

**Serves 2**

## WHITE ASPARAGUS WITH BROWN BUTTER SAUCE

8 white asparagus
juice of ½ lemon
1 bay leaf

**For the sauce**
small bunch of flat-leaf parsley
1 hard-boiled egg, finely chopped
½ white onion, finely diced
100g butter
juice of ½ lemon
sea salt and freshly ground black
    pepper

**La Rioja is the wine capital of Spain, but it's also home to some amazing food. There's a big tapas culture in the region and everywhere you look there are people eating and drinking. White asparagus are grown underground with no light, which prevents the plant from producing chlorophyll and turning green. This beautifully easy vegetarian dish lets it shine as the star of the show.**

Bring a large pan of salted water to the boil. Using a potato peeler, peel top to bottom all around the asparagus, then chop the tails off. Add to the boiling water with the lemon juice and bay leaf and cook for 6–8 minutes until a knife can pierce through the asparagus.

Chop the parsley and mix with the egg and onion.

Heat the butter to a nut brown colour, add the lemon juice and egg mixture, season and stir through.

To serve, drain the asparagus, pop onto plates and spoon over the sauce.

# CEPS WITH BAYONNE HAM

4 ceps
drizzle of olive oil
4 slices of Bayonne ham, to serve

### For the dressing
3 tablespoons olive oil
1 tablespoon sherry vinegar
1 tablespoon chopped flat-leaf parsley
sea salt and freshly ground black
    pepper

**This simple dish of mushrooms smothered in a delicious dressing, finished with some chopped ham, celebrates brilliant local Riojan produce.**

If you want to BBQ the ceps, heat a BBQ until hot and the coals are white.

Slice the ceps into four pieces, drizzle with olive oil, then pop onto the BBQ and cook for 2–3 minutes until charred on one side. Flip over and repeat. Alternatively, you can cook the ceps in a frying pan on the hob.

Meanwhile, mix all the dressing ingredients together and season well.

To serve, pile the mushrooms onto plates, spoon over the dressing and top with the ham.

# CALAMARI WITH SALSA AND AIOLI

**Serves 2**

---

750ml olive oil, for frying

750ml vegetable oil, for frying

2 large squid, cleaned and cut
    into rings

200ml full-fat milk

100g plain flour, seasoned

sea salt and freshly ground
    black pepper

lemon wedges, to serve

**For the aioli**

1 garlic bulb

200ml olive oil, plus extra
    for drizzling

3 egg yolks

1 tablespoon Dijon mustard

pinch of saffron, soaked in a splash
    of hot water

squeeze of lemon juice

**For the salsa**

1 green pepper

½ onion

1 garlic clove

50ml olive oil

zest and juice of ½ lemon

4 small, dried chillies, crushed

**A classic dish of lightly battered squid rings, served alongside a roasted garlic and saffron aioli for dipping and a gorgeous green salsa for freshness with a bit of heat from the chillies. This is the perfect way to enjoy fresh seafood.**

Heat a BBQ until hot and the coals are white or preheat the oven to 160°C (140°C fan)/325°F/gas 3.

For the aioli, cut the top off the garlic bulb, place into a foil parcel, drizzle with oil, then pop on the coals and roast for 10 minutes. If cooking in the oven, roast for 40 minutes. Unwrap the foil, squeeze out the cloves and leave to cool.

To make the mayo, whisk the egg yolks and mustard together slowly, then drizzle in the oil, whisking continuously until thick. Finish by mixing in the saffron, roasted garlic and lemon juice.

To make the salsa, chop the pepper, onion and garlic together until fine. Mix in the oil and lemon zest and juice. Stir through the crushed chillies and season.

Heat both oils to 180°C (350°F) in a deep-sided saucepan.

Coat the squid rings in the milk and then dip into the seasoned flour. Deep-fry in batches for 1–2 minutes, drain on kitchen paper and season with salt.

To serve, spoon the aioli into a small bowl, put the salsa into another small bowl and pile up the calamari on a serving dish with lemon wedges for squeezing over.

# MUSSEL SOUP

**Serves 4–6**

---

50ml olive oil

4 garlic cloves, crushed

100ml white wine

2 bay leaves

a few flat-leaf parsley stalks

2kg mussels, cleaned and debearded

rind of 1 orange

### For the soup

2 garlic cloves, chopped

50ml olive oil

100g chorizo, diced

zest and juice of 1 orange

200g chickpeas, cooked

2 teaspoons red pepper paste

2 roasted red peppers from a
   jar, sliced

½ teaspoon sea salt

a few sprigs of flat-leaf parsley,
   chopped

**Mussel farming is a significant part of the economy and culture of Rías Baixas, Galicia. The mussels are farmed on rafts in the region's inlets and estuaries and then harvested and used in a variety of dishes, including this ultimate soup for mussel fans.**

If you want to cook on the BBQ, heat a BBQ until hot and the coals are white.

Place a large pan with a lid over the heat and heat the oil, then add the garlic and cook for a minute. Add the wine, bay leaves, parsley stalks, mussels and orange rind. Pop the lid on and cook for 3–4 minutes until all the mussels are open. Drain the mussels, discarding any that have not opened and keeping all the cooking liquor. Pick three-quarters of the mussels out of their shells.

For the soup, place the pan back onto the heat, add the garlic and oil and cook for a minute. Then add the chorizo, orange zest and juice, chickpeas, red pepper paste and sliced peppers, give it all a big stir, then pour in the reserved mussel cooking liquor, being careful not to add any of the sediment. Bring to the boil, then reduce for 2–3 minutes. Pop the mussels back in the pan to warm through, including the ones in the shells. Season with the salt and sprinkle over the parsley.

Spoon into bowls to serve.

# PINTXOS

## GILDA Serves 2

8 green olives
8 salted anchovies
8 guindilla peppers
olive oil, for drizzling (optional)

**Pintxos (peen-chos) are the Basque country's answer to tapas, made especially famous by the world-renowned food scene of San Sebastián. Pintxos are typically finger foods, usually small enough to be eaten in just one or two bites. This fabulous pintxo dish doesn't even need any cooking – simply skewer up an olive, an anchovy and a pickled pepper. Perfect.**

On each skewer, add an olive, then an anchovy, curling it through the skewer. Finish with a pepper, and drizzle with olive oil if desired.

## TOMATOES ON TOAST Serves 4

50ml olive oil
8 slices of baguette
8 tomatoes
1 garlic clove
8 white brined anchovies, for topping (optional)
sea salt and freshly ground black pepper

**Txikiteo is the Basque culture of going out for pintxos. You have a small drink and one or two pintxos in each bar, before moving on to the next. Pintxos are usually eaten as a snack to keep you going before a main meal, but while there are some fantastic restaurants in San Sebastián, nothing beats a good pintxo crawl that lasts a whole evening. This pintxos plate showcases wonderful Spanish tomatoes. Keep it simple and delicious as it is, or top with anchovies to change it up.**

Drizzle half the olive oil over the bread and toast on the BBQ for 1–2 minutes until charred. Alternatively, toast the bread in a griddle pan on the hob.

For the topping, halve the tomatoes and grate over a sieve and bowl with a box grater. Crush the garlic with a little salt until it resembles a fine paste, then mix into the tomato pulp with the remaining olive oil. (You can use the juice for stock or a Bloody Mary.)

Spoon the tomato mixture onto the toasts and top with an anchovy if desired.

# COSTA BLANCA TUNA SALAD WITH ROASTED VEGETABLES

**Serves 2**

---

1 large spring onion

2 red peppers, cored, deseeded and halved

bunch of asparagus

100ml olive oil

1 aubergine, sliced

1 large courgette, sliced

1 teaspoon cumin seeds

1 teaspoon coriander seeds

25g almonds

1 tablespoon sherry vinegar

½ teaspoon pimentón ahumado (smoked paprika)

2 x 200g tuna steaks

4 tablespoons honey

1 frisée or lollo rosso lettuce, leaves separated

3 hard-boiled eggs, halved

sea salt

**The Costa Blanca boasts over 200 kilometres of coastline in the province of Alicante, where the traditional food revolves around the Mediterranean Sea, from which its finest ingredients originate. This tuna salad stars one of those delicacies. BBQ the tuna alongside a variety of colourful veggies and serve them mixed with some hard-boiled eggs, salad leaves and a delicious spicy, nutty dressing.**

Heat a BBQ until hot and the coals are white or preheat the oven to 200°C (180°C fan)/400°F/gas 6.

Place the spring onion, red peppers and asparagus on a baking tray, drizzle with olive oil and cook on the BBQ for 3–4 minutes until charred. Pop into a bowl, then do the same with the aubergine and courgette. Alternatively, cook all the vegetables together in the oven for 15–20 minutes until charred. Season with salt.

Toast the cumin and coriander seeds and the almonds in a small frying pan over a medium heat for 30 seconds, then pop into a pestle and mortar and pound. Spoon into a bowl, then mix with the sherry vinegar, 50ml of the oil, ½ teaspoon of salt and the pimentón.

Seal the tuna on all sides in a very hot pan with a drizzle of olive oil for 1 minute. Roll the tuna in 2 tablespoons of the honey, then the almond spice mix and slice.

To serve, pile the vegetables onto a platter, top with lettuce and dot with the hard-boiled eggs and sliced tuna. Spoon over the remaining almond spice mix and drizzle over the remaining honey.

# DEEP-FRIED AUBERGINES

**Serves 2**

---

1.5 litres vegetable oil, for frying
1½ aubergines, sliced
honey, to serve

**For the batter**
150g gluten-free self-raising flour
100ml cider

**For the sauce**
50ml olive oil
2 garlic cloves, chopped
2 bay leaves
3 large tomatoes, grated
pinch of pimentón ahumado
 (smoked paprika)
sea salt and freshly ground black
 pepper

**Fried aubergines drizzled with honey is a classic tapas dish served in bars throughout Spain. Here I've also added a fresh tomato sauce to take it to another level.**

Put all the ingredients for the sauce into a pan and bring to the boil. Then reduce by half, season, stir and remove from the heat. Set aside.

In a medium saucepan, heat the oil to 170°C (340°F).

In a large bowl, whisk the flour and cider together. In batches, dip the aubergines in the batter, then deep-fry for 2 minutes. Drain on kitchen paper and season with salt.

To serve, spoon the sauce into the middle of a plate, top with the deep-fried aubergines and drizzle over some honey.

# CASTILE AND LEÓN GARLIC SOUP WITH CHEESY CROUTONS

**Serves 4**

50ml olive oil

6 garlic cloves, sliced

50g lardo, diced

50ml white wine

1 teaspoon pimentón ahumado
    (smoked paprika)

1 egg

100g Serrano ham, diced

sea salt and freshly ground black
    pepper

### For the stock

600g chicken wings, skin on

2 bay leaves

6 black peppercorns

### For the croutons

4 thick slices of white bread

50ml olive oil

200g Tetilla cheese, peeled and sliced
    (or mozzarella if you can't get
    hold of Tetilla)

**One of the most traditional recipes of Castile and León is sopa de ajo or Castilian garlic soup. A peasant-style dish, often made by shepherds, it is cooked to help combat the region's cold winters. Garlic and leftover bread are used and eggs are sometimes added. It is even said to be a hangover cure…**

Place all the ingredients for the stock into a pan, cover with water and bring to the boil. Reduce the heat and simmer for 1 hour. Remove from the heat, strain and set aside. You are aiming to have about 1 litre of stock.

If you want to use a BBQ for the soup, heat a BBQ until hot and the coals are white.

For the soup, add half the oil, the garlic and lardo to a small frying pan and gently fry for 2 minutes to soften. Add the wine and pimentón, cook out for a minute, then ladle in 1 litre of the chicken stock. Bring to the boil, then reduce the heat and simmer for 10 minutes. Season, then whisk in the egg.

For the croutons, drizzle the bread with the oil, then toast on the BBQ. Alternatively, you can toast the bread in a frying pan on the hob. Dip one side of two pieces of toast in the soup, then top with the cheese. Sit the other slices of toast on top, then toast until the cheese is melting. Cut into squares and pop in the soup to serve.

Garnish with the diced Serrano ham and drizzle over the remaining olive oil.

# CROQUETAS WITH HAM, ALMONDS AND MANCHEGO

**Serves 4**

100g butter
250g plain flour
500ml full-fat milk
100g Manchego, cubed
2 tablespoons chopped almonds
100g Serrano ham, diced
2 eggs, beaten
100g breadcrumbs
1.5 litres vegetable oil, for deep-frying
sea salt and freshly ground black pepper
50g aged Manchego, to serve

**These croquetas contain one of Spain's most famous culinary exports: queso manchego. This cheese is made in the La Mancha region from the milk of the Manchega sheep. It is aged between 60 days and 2 years and has a buttery texture, often containing small, unevenly distributed air pockets. Here I've combined it with ham and almonds for the perfect croqueta filling.**

Put the butter into a pan over a medium heat and, when foaming, add 150g of the flour and cook for a couple of minutes. Whisk in the milk and cook gently over a very low heat for 3 minutes, stirring constantly.

Remove the mixture from the heat and leave it to cool for a few minutes. Then beat in the Manchego, ½ teaspoon of salt and some black pepper to taste. Cover with clingfilm and chill the mixture in the fridge for 2 hours.

Remove the mixture from the fridge and divide it in half. Mix half with the almonds and half with the ham. Shape into 8–10 sausage shapes.

Put the remaining 100g flour, egg and breadcrumbs in three separate bowls. Coat the croquetas first in the flour, then dip in the egg and finally coat in the breadcrumbs.

Heat the oil to 180°C (350°F) in a deep-sided saucepan. Drop the croquetas into the hot oil and cook for 1–2 minutes until crisp and golden, working in batches. Drain on kitchen paper and serve immediately, with the aged Manchego grated over the top.

# CARPACCIO OF SEA BASS WITH CAVIAR

**Serves 2**

2 x 200g sea bass fillets, skinned

1 avocado

2 limes

¼ mango, finely diced

2 slices of tomato, finely diced

¼ red chilli, diced

a few mint and coriander leaves, chopped

pinch of sea salt

50ml olive oil

**To serve**

3 teaspoons caviar

a few sprigs of dill

**Make sure you use the freshest possible sea bass for this carpaccio. Like a Peruvian ceviche, we're using the lime juice to very briefly 'cook' the fish and then serving it with quenelles of an almost guacamole-like avocado mixture, teaspoons of caviar and dill. Art on a plate.**

Thinly slice the sea bass and place on a tray.

Pass the avocado through a sieve into a bowl, add the zest and juice from 1 lime, stir, then mix in the mango, tomato, chilli and herbs. Squeeze the remaining lime over the fish and season with the salt. Drizzle over the olive oil and leave for 2 minutes.

To serve, cover a large sharing plate with the fish slices, top with quenelles of avocado mixture and the caviar and dot with sprigs of dill.

# SALT-BAKED CELERIAC AND NEW POTATOES WITH SALSA

**Serves 6**

500g plain flour, plus extra
    for dusting

500g sea salt

1 large celeriac, trimmed
    so the base is flat

500g small potatoes

30cm piece of rope

olive oil, for drizzling

### For the salsa

1 red pepper, roasted and chopped

1 garlic clove, crushed

pinch of cumin seeds

100g tomato pulp

**This is a great vegetarian dish. The celeriac and new potatoes are both baked in their own salt dough parcels so they gently steam in their own juices to give tender veg, which I've then served with a fresh tomato and red pepper salsa.**

Preheat the oven to 200°C (180°C fan)/400°F/gas 6.

Mix the flour, salt and enough water to bring the ingredients together in a ball of dough. On a lightly floured surface, roll out half the dough into a 5mm thick circle. Place the celeriac in the centre of the dough circle and pull up the dough to cover and seal. With the remaining pastry, make another circle and pop in the potatoes. Seal and make a lid, so that it looks like a parcel. Tie the rope around the top, then place the potato and celeriac parcels onto a lined baking tray and bake for 1 hour 10 minutes.

Mix all the ingredients for the salsa together in a small bowl.

Carefully cut away the crust around the celeriac. To serve, cut the celeriac into thin slices, sit on a plate and drizzle with olive oil. Open up the potato parcel and serve with the salsa.

# TAPAS 3 WAYS

**Serves 4**

### For the chicken

16 skin-on, bone-in chicken wings

50ml olive oil

1 lemon, sliced

2 tablespoons honey

1 tablespoon sherry vinegar

a few sprigs of flat-leaf parsley,
  chopped

pinch of pimentón ahumado
  (smoked paprika)

### For the gambas pil pil

16 prawns, peeled

pinch of salt

pinch of chilli flakes

rind of 1 lemon

1 garlic bulb, roasted

100ml olive oil

pinch of pimentón ahumado
  (smoked paprika)

sea salt

### For the anchovies

18 boquerones

1 lemon, segmented

1 garlic clove

pinch of salt

a few sprigs of flat-leaf parsley,
  chopped

100ml olive oil

baguette, to serve

**Not one but three delicious tapas dishes! Gambas pil pil is a traditional tapas dish, originating from the Basque region, while boquerones are fresh anchovies, as opposed to the heavily salted variety. Here the boquerones are inspired by the classic boquerones en vinagre, where they are served with a dressing of vinegar, olive oil, garlic and parsley. The chicken is roasted in honey, vinegar, pimentón and lemon and served scattered with parsley for a smoky, sweet, spicy flavour.**

If using a BBQ, heat a BBQ until hot and the coals are white. Preheat the oven to 200°C (180°C fan)/400°F/gas 6 or heat a pizza oven to 400°C (750°F).

Start by making the chicken. On a metal tray, roll the chicken wings in the oil and lemon pieces and season with salt. Roast in the oven for 20 minutes, or the pizza oven for 10 minutes, then finish with the honey, vinegar, parsley and pimentón. Roll the chicken around again on the tray, then pop the tray on the BBQ or hob to reduce until the sauce is sticky.

For the gambas pil pil, divide the prawns into two ovenproof dishes. Season with the salt, pop in the chilli flakes, lemon rind and roasted garlic and cover in the oil and pimentón. Roast in the oven for 8 minutes, or in the pizza oven for 2–3 minutes.

For the anchovies, lay the boquerones onto a plate. Then, in a pestle and mortar, pound the lemon, garlic and salt together. Add the parsley and olive oil and mix through. Spoon over the boquerones and serve alongside the chicken and prawns, with slices of baguette.

# EMPANADAS

**Serves 6–8/Makes 12**

---

**For the pastry**

500g plain flour, plus extra
     for dusting
200g salted butter, cubed
1 teaspoon salt
2 teaspoons white wine vinegar
1 egg, beaten for egg wash

**For the filling**

1kg mussels, cooked and meat
     removed (250g cooked weight)
250g pork mince, fried
12 slices of Tetilla cheese

**For the sauce**

100g tomato pulp
2 green peppers, cored, deseeded
     and chopped
1 bay leaf
2 garlic cloves
pinch of chilli flakes

**Empanadas are classic Spanish pastry turnovers, which are baked or fried and filled with a range of delicious fillings. Here I've given you not one but two tasty options – mussels and minced pork, both combined with Tetilla, a cow's milk cheese from Galicia.**

Start by making the sauce. Fry all the ingredients together for 5 minutes, then split into two bowls. Add the cooked mussels to one bowl and the cooked pork mince to the other and give both mixtures a big stir. Leave to cool.

Place all the pastry ingredients and 75ml water into a freestanding mixer fitted with the K attachment and mix until the dough comes together in a ball. Pop into a bowl, cover and leave to rest at room temperature for 1 hour.

Preheat the oven to 200°C (180°C fan)/400°F/gas 6.

Roll out the pastry on a lightly floured work surface. Cut out twelve 12cm circles using a saucer as a guide. Place a slice of cheese on each circle of dough, then top six with the mussel filling and six with the pork mixture. Fold over and press the edges of the pastries together. Crimp the edges with your fingers. Pop onto a lined baking tray, then egg wash and bake for 25 minutes until puffed up and golden.

# BAKED ARTICHOKES AND EGGS

**Serves 4**

---

5 purple artichokes
100ml olive oil
1 bay leaf
4 eggs
crusty bread, to serve

**For the sauce**
3 large tomatoes
50ml olive oil
1 onion, diced
3 garlic cloves, diced
1 charred red pepper, cored,
    deseeded and sliced
1 teaspoon pimentón ahumado
    (smoked paprika)
½ teaspoon sea salt

**This dish is my personal celebration of locally grown Spanish vegetables. Perfect for brunch or lunch served with crusty bread for dipping. Delicious.**

Heat a BBQ until hot and the coals are white. Preheat the oven to 200°C (180°C fan)/400°F/gas 6 or heat a pizza oven to 300°C (570°F).

Start by prepping the artichokes. Peel away the bottom leaves and then, using a potato peeler, trim the stems back. Remove the top third of each artichoke with a knife and then cut into sixths. Pop the artichokes into a pan with 100ml water, the oil and bay leaf and cook for 15 minutes until all the liquid has gone.

Grate the tomatoes over a sieve with a box grater. Chop the skins finely and mix up with the pulp and juice.

Heat the olive oil in a pan over a medium heat, then add the onion and garlic and cook for 2–3 minutes to soften. Add the tomatoes, pepper and pimentón and bring to the boil. Reduce by half and season with the salt.

Put the artichokes into an ovenproof dish, spoon over the sauce and crack the eggs on top. Place into the oven and bake for 10 minutes, or the pizza oven for 6–8 minutes. Serve with crusty bread.

# SPANISH FISH SOUP

**Serves 8**

2 litres fish stock

10 large prawns

1 red mullet

1 medium sea bass

3 large tomatoes

50ml olive oil, plus extra for drizzling

1 bulb garlic, halved

1 onion, diced

1 green pepper, cored, deseeded
    and diced

2 celery sticks, diced

200g cooked cannellini beans

1 teaspoon pimentón ahumado
    (smoked paprika)

2 tablespoons sherry

300g clams, cleaned

200g mussels, cleaned and debearded

sea salt and freshly ground black
    pepper

**This soup makes the most of the wonderful array of fish and seafood on offer along Spain's coastline. With two types of fish alongside prawns, mussels and clams, this a seafood lover's dream.**

If you want to cook this on a BBQ, heat a BBQ until hot and the coals are white.

Warm the fish stock in a large pan. Peel the prawns and pop the shells into the fish stock. Remove the head and fins from the mullet and sea bass and pop into the fish stock. Cut the fish into 2cm chunks through the bone and pop to one side.

Grate the tomatoes over a sieve with a box grater and add the skins to the stock. Bring to the boil and simmer for 10 minutes.

Place a large paella pan onto a medium heat, add the oil and all the vegetables and cook for 2–3 minutes to soften. Then add the tomato pulp and juice, bring to the boil and reduce by a third. Add the cannellini beans and pimentón, then ladle in the stock through a sieve. Add the sherry and season. Bring to the boil, then pop in the sea bass, red mullet and clams and cook for 4–5 minutes. Then add the prawns and mussels and cook for 3 minutes or until all the mussels have opened (discard any that haven't).

Ladle into bowls and drizzle with olive oil to serve.

# SPICED AUBERGINES

**Serves 6**

---

3 aubergines

5 long aubergines

100ml olive oil

1 teaspoon coriander seeds

1 teaspoon cumin seeds

150ml Greek yogurt

2 tablespoons tahini

50g almonds, fried in olive oil

1 garlic clove

zest and juice of 1 lime, plus extra
lime halves to serve

1 teaspoon each white and black
sesame seeds

2 tablespoons honey

a few sprigs of mint and flat-leaf
parsley, chopped

seeds of ½ pomegranate

sea salt and freshly ground black
pepper

**Smoky charred aubergines with a spicy, sweet dressing, piled atop a bed of creamy tahini yogurt. Served with mint, parsley and pomegranate seeds for freshness and toasted sesame seeds for a little crunch, this is a delicious veggie BBQ option for vegetarians and carnivores alike.**

If you want to use the BBQ, heat a BBQ until hot and the coals are white.

Prick the aubergines all over with a fork, then cut the big ones in half. Drizzle over half the oil and season with 1 teaspoon of salt. Pop onto the BBQ and cook for 4–5 minutes until charred on both sides. Alternatively, grill in the oven on high on both sides for 3–4 minutes.

Toast the coriander and cumin seeds in a small frying pan for a couple of minutes until fragrant. Then pound together in a pestle and mortar until quite fine. Sprinkle half the spices onto the cooked aubergines, then season.

Mix the yogurt and tahini together until well combined.

Add the almonds and garlic to the remaining spices and pound to a quite coarse paste. Add the remaining oil and the lime zest and juice and mix together.

Lightly toast the sesame seeds in a dry frying pan for 1 minute.

To serve, spoon the tahini yogurt all over a platter, top with the aubergines, spoon over the spiced almond oil and sprinkle over the toasted sesame seeds. Drizzle with the honey, then sprinkle over the herbs and pomegranate seeds and serve with lime halves for squeezing over.

# BBQ QUEENIE SCALLOPS, MUSSELS, BABY SQUID AND PRAWNS WITH A RED PEPPER DRESSING

**Serves 6**

12 mussels, cleaned and debearded

12 baby squid

olive oil, for drizzling

juice of ½ lemon

2 garlic cloves, crushed

2 tablespoons red pepper paste

a few sprigs of flat-leaf parsley, plus extra, chopped, to garnish

50g butter, softened

8 prawns, shelled and chopped

12 queenie scallops, cleaned and roes attached

sea salt and freshly ground black pepper

**Seafood on a BBQ is easy and quick. So fire it up and enjoy a feast of the best of Spain's seafood – scallops dotted with a prawn and mussel butter, alongside squid in a red pepper dressing.**

Heat a BBQ until hot and the coals are white.

Place the mussels onto the BBQ rack and cook for 3–4 minutes until fully opened, then remove the meat and discard the shells. (Discard any that have not opened.)

Drizzle the baby squid in oil and the lemon juice, season, then place onto the BBQ rack and cook for 2 minutes, turning until charred all over.

To make the dressing, mix the garlic and red pepper paste with a glug of olive oil, season, then mix in the parsley.

Pop the squid onto a platter, then spoon over half the dressing.

Mix the butter with the remaining dressing, then add the prawns and mussel meat and give it all a good mix until well combined.

Pop the scallops onto the BBQ rack, dot with the prawn and mussel butter and cook for 2 minutes until hot and bubbling. Place onto a platter and sprinkle with parsley to serve.

# SANTIAGO MUSSELS AND RICE

## Serves 4

---

50ml olive oil

1 onion, diced

3 garlic cloves, chopped

3 soft chorizo, sliced

200g bomba rice

150ml dry cider

500ml red shellfish stock

1 teaspoon pimentón ahumado (smoked paprika)

8 padrón peppers

12 small roasted pimento peppers, sliced

12 large mussels, cleaned and debearded

a few sprigs of flat-leaf parsley, chopped

sea salt

**Santiago de Compostela is the capital of northwest Spain's Galicia region. This area is the most important producer of mussels in Europe, with over 3,000 mussel rafts in the region's inlets and estuaries. The farming process involves suspending ropes from rafts, which the mussels attach themselves to and feed on the phytoplankton in the water. Here they're combined with rice, another of Spain's top culinary exports.**

Heat a large paella pan over a medium heat, splash in the oil, then add the onion and garlic and cook for 2 minutes to soften. Pop in the chorizo and fry for another 2 minutes, then pour in the rice, cider and 250ml of the stock. Add the pimentón, give it all a big stir, then season with salt and cook for 10 minutes. Add 125ml of the stock and the padrón and pimento peppers and cook for another 5 minutes.

Finally, pop in the mussels and the remaining 125ml stock and cook for 5 minutes until the mussels have fully opened.

Discard any mussels that haven't opened, sprinkle over the parsley and serve.

# CLAMS WITH SAMPHIRE

**Serves 2**

---

2 garlic cloves, crushed
50ml olive oil
50ml white wine
500g clams, cleaned
50g samphire
juice of ½ lemon
small bunch of flat-leaf parsley
pinch of sea salt
4 slices of baguette, fried

*Salicornia*, better known as samphire or sea asparagus, is nourished by the saline water of the Cádiz Bay, where they have 39 hectares of salt marshes and marshes to collect this delicacy. *Salicornia* is a halophyte plant, adapted to live in saline environments. Here we've harvested it and combined it with local clams in a lemony garlic broth.

Heat a BBQ until hot and the coals are white. Alternatively, you can cook the dish on the hob.

In a large pan over a medium heat, cook the garlic in 25ml of the oil for 1 minute. Add the wine and clams and cook for 2 minutes until all the clams have opened. Stir through the samphire, lemon juice and remaining 25ml oil.

Chop the parsley, then add to the clams and season with the salt. Discard any unopened clams.

Dot with the bread to serve.

# ZARZUELA

**Serves 10**

---

### For the rice

75ml olive oil

4 garlic cloves, crushed

100g lardo, sliced

200g Ibérico ham, diced

6 butifarra sausages

3 large tomatoes

1 onion, sliced

1 green pepper, cored, deseeded
and cut into chunks

1 teaspoon pimentón ahumado
(smoked paprika), plus a pinch

pinch of saffron

1 teaspoon dried oregano

400g bomba rice

5 x 150g pieces of cod, cut through
the bone

6 large clams, cleaned

12 medium clams, cleaned

10 mussels, cleaned and debearded

6 scallops

200g small clams, cleaned

1 giant red prawn

3 red prawns

12 shrimp

3 langoustines

2 octopus tentacles, cooked

a few sprigs of flat-leaf parsley,
chopped

sea salt

### For the stock

1 small crab

6 small fish (I used a mix of grey and
red mullet)

1 bay leaf

**Catalonian zarzuela is aptly named after a genre of Spanish musical theatre that blends many contrasting styles of music and dance, as this dish combines seafood, fish, sausage, rice and vegetables to give a flavour of Spain in just one dish.**

If using a BBQ, heat a BBQ until hot and the coals are white.

Pop all the ingredients for the stock into a large pan and add enough water to cover. Bring to the boil, then simmer for 20 minutes. Drain the stock and discard the crab, fish and bay leaf. You are aiming to have 1.2 litres of stock.

For the rice, heat a very large paella pan over a high heat. Pour in half the oil, then add the garlic, lardo and Ibérico ham and cook for 2 minutes. Add the sausages and cook until browned.

Grate the tomatoes over a sieve with a box grater and pop the skins into the stock and the juice and pulp into the paella pan. Add the onion, pepper, pimentón and saffron to the paella pan and give it all a big stir. Pour in 900ml of the stock and bring to the boil. Sprinkle over the oregano and rice and cook over a medium heat for 8 minutes.

Sit the cod pieces in the mixture and cook for 3 minutes. Flip over the cod pieces, nestle the large clams in the rice and cook for a further 5 minutes. Add the medium clams, mussels and scallops to the rice and season with salt. Give it all a gentle stir, then cook for 3 minutes. Scatter over the small clams, pour in the remaining 300ml stock and cook for 2 minutes until all the clams have opened. Remove from the heat, discarding any unopened clams, and leave to rest.

Place the grill rack onto the BBQ, drizzle the prawns, shrimp and langoustines with oil and cook for 2–3 minutes. Mix the pinch of pimentón with a little oil and brush over the octopus. Cook on the BBQ for 3 minutes, turning until charred. Or you can cook these in a griddle or frying pan on the hob.

To serve, sit the shellfish on top of the rice with the octopus, sprinkle over the parsley and drizzle with the rest of the oil.

# CASA MONTAÑA SQUID

**Serves 2**

---

4 medium squid, cleaned

25ml olive oil

pinch of salt

juice of ½ lemon

sprinkle of phytoplankton powder,
    to serve (available in health food
    stores – optional)

### For the salsa

2 long green peppers

50ml olive oil

1 teaspoon cumin seeds

1 garlic clove

a few sprigs of parsley, chopped

juice of 1 lemon

sea salt

### For the dressing

50ml balsamic vinegar

1 tablespoon caster sugar

1 teaspoon sherry

**This dish was inspired by my trip to Casa Montaña restaurant in Valencia, where apparently nothing has changed since its founding in 1836. It continues to be a meeting place that opens the door to a universe of sensations.**

If using a BBQ, heat a BBQ until hot and the coals are white.

For the salsa, cut the peppers into chunks and remove the seeds. Drizzle over the olive oil, then pop the peppers onto the BBQ rack to char and soften for 3–4 minutes. Alternatively, cook in a grill pan on the hob. Remove the peppers from the heat and chop into smaller pieces.

Toast the cumin seeds in a small pan for 30 seconds, then crush the garlic with a pinch of salt in a pestle and mortar. Add the cumin and parsley to the pestle and mortar and pound again, then pop in the peppers and pound until a thick paste forms. Finish with the lemon juice and season with salt.

For the dressing, pour the vinegar, sugar and sherry into a pan and bring to the boil. Then reduce by three-quarters. Remove from the heat and leave to cool slightly.

Roll the squid in the oil and salt, then put directly onto the BBQ rack and cook for a minute. Flip over and cook for another minute. Cook the tentacles for 1 minute only, then squeeze the lemon juice all over the squid. Alternatively, you can cook the squid in a grill pan on the hob.

To serve, spoon the green salsa onto a platter, drizzle with the dressing, then top with the squid and sprinkle over the phytoplankton powder, if using.

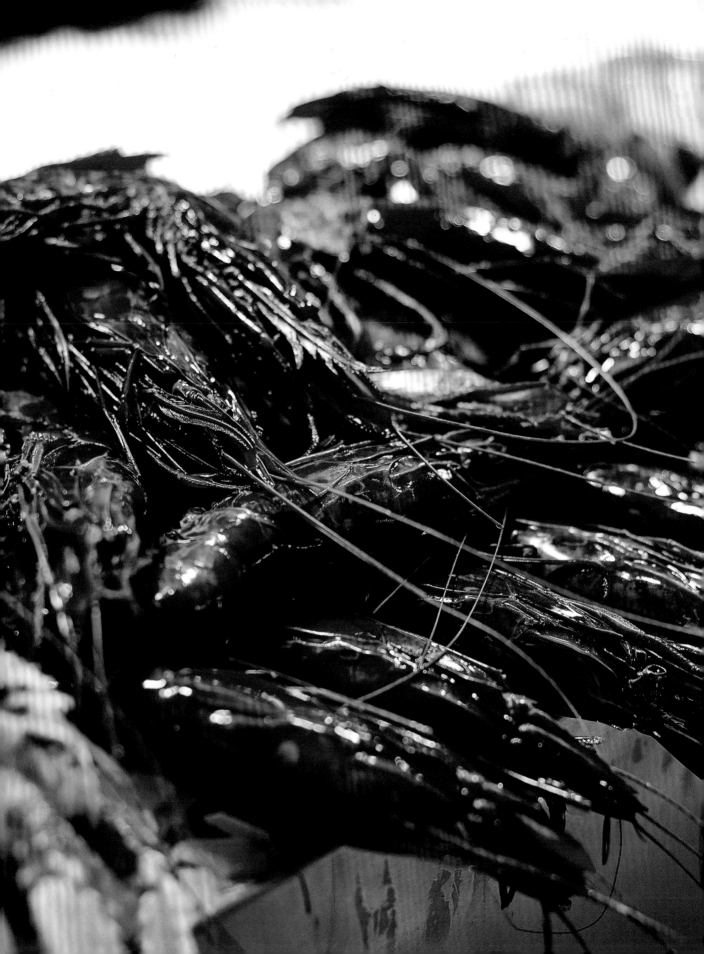

# ALICANTE RICE WITH RABBIT AND RED PRAWNS

**Serves 6**

75ml olive oil

1 red pepper, cored, deseeded and quartered

1 green pepper, cored, deseeded and quartered

2 large spring onions, sliced lengthways

2 large tomatoes

750ml hot chicken stock

1 rabbit, cut into 8 portions

2 garlic cloves, crushed

200g soft chorizo, sliced

450g bomba rice

pinch of pimentón ahumado (smoked paprika)

pinch of saffron

3 bay leaves

sea salt

a few sprigs of flat-leaf parsley, chopped, to garnish

### To serve
10 Dénia red prawns

drizzle of olive oil (optional)

**This dish features two of Alicante's most notable ingredients – the famous red prawn of Dénia and rice. The Dénia prawn is particularly juicy and its reddish colour is more intense than other varieties. There are four categories according to their size. The largest, category 1, is the most coveted and the most expensive.**

Heat a BBQ until hot and the coals are white. Alternatively, you can cook the dish on the hob.

Drizzle a little of the olive oil over the peppers and spring onions and cook on the BBQ for 2–3 minutes until just charred or use a frying pan on the hob. Transfer onto a tray.

Meanwhile, grate the tomatoes over a sieve with a box grater and pop the skins into the chicken stock.

Heat a paella pan until hot, add the remaining oil and fry the rabbit on both sides for 3–4 minutes until coloured. Pop in the garlic, chorizo, tomato juice and pulp, and rice and give it a stir. Then add three-quarters of the stock. Sprinkle over the pimentón and saffron, pop in the bay leaves and simmer for 8 minutes.

Chop up the peppers, then add to the pan along with the spring onions. Season with salt, add a ladleful of chicken stock, then cook for another 8 minutes. Add the last ladle of stock, then remove from the heat and leave to rest.

Place the prawns onto the BBQ rack and cook for 1 minute on each side. Alternatively, you can cook the prawns in a grill pan on the hob. Transfer to a plate, season with salt and drizzle over olive oil if desired.

To serve, spoon the rabbit, rice and vegetables onto a plate and sit the prawns alongside. Garnish with the parsley.

# WHITE BEAN AND OCTOPUS SEAFOOD STEW

**Serves 4**

---

4 octopus tentacles

pinch of pimentón ahumado (smoked paprika)

50ml olive oil

2 bay leaves

1 garlic clove, crushed

1 sprig of rosemary

juice of ½ lemon

**For the stew**

3 garlic cloves, chopped

25ml olive oil

3 bay leaves

1 sprig of rosemary, leaves picked

1 large tomato, diced

300ml chicken stock

200g cooked fabas de Lourenza (Galician long white beans) or another white bean, such as cannellini, if you can't get hold of these

300g clams

8 queenie scallops

a few sprigs of flat-leaf parsley, chopped

**This dish uses faba de Lourenza (a type of Galician long white bean), which are delicious and buttery, perfect for making Spanish stews. Here I've combined them with another iconic Galician ingredient and common catch for local fishermen: octopus.**

If you want to BBQ the octopus, heat a BBQ until hot and the coals are white.

Marinate the octopus in the pimentón, olive oil, bay leaves, garlic, rosemary and lemon juice for 5 minutes.

To make the stew, in a paella pan over a medium heat, fry the garlic in the olive oil for 1 minute, then add the bay leaves, rosemary and tomato, give it all a stir and add one-third of the stock. Bring to the boil, then reduce the heat and simmer for 2–3 minutes until the tomato is just starting to break down. Pop in the beans and the remaining stock, bring to the boil again, then add the clams and sit the scallops in the stew. Season with salt and cook for 3–4 minutes until all the shellfish has fully opened (discard any that haven't opened).

Meanwhile, pop the octopus onto the BBQ and cook for 3–4 minutes until charred, brushing with the pimentón oil and turning occasionally. Alternatively, you can cook the octopus in a frying pan on the hob.

Sit the octopus on top of the stew, finish with the chopped parsley and serve.

# BLACK RICE AND SQUID BALLS

**Serves 6**

---

50ml olive oil

2 garlic cloves, crushed

½ onion, diced

1 large tomato, grated (4 tablespoons)

½ teaspoon dried oregano

200g bomba rice

500ml fish stock

2 x 8g sachets squid ink

1 large squid, diced

75g Parmesan, grated

1.5 litres vegetable oil, for frying

100g plain flour

2 eggs

150g dried breadcrumbs

150ml crème fraîche, to serve

### For the butter balls

1 garlic bulb

drizzle of olive oil

100g butter, softened

### For the sauce

25ml olive oil

1 garlic clove, crushed

100g tomato pulp

pinch of dried oregano

2 roasted red peppers, sliced

½ teaspoon sea salt

1 tablespoon sherry vinegar

**This dish features the classic pairing of squid and black rice, but here it's shaped into balls, coated with breadcrumbs and fried – similar to Italian arancini. Serve with a red pepper and tomato sauce, topped with a dollop of crème fraîche. Delicious.**

Heat a BBQ until hot and the coals are white or preheat the oven to 180°C (160°C fan)/350°F/gas 4.

To make the risotto, heat a large paella pan over a medium heat. Pour in the oil, then fry the garlic with the onion for a minute. Spoon in the tomato pulp and oregano, add the rice and coat with the oil mixture. Pour in the stock, bring to the boil and then add the squid ink. Reduce the heat and simmer for 10 minutes. To finish, add the squid and cook for a further 4 minutes. Stir through the Parmesan and leave to cool.

To make the butter balls, cut the top fifth off the garlic, pop in a foil parcel, drizzle with olive oil and seal. Roast in the coals of the BBQ for 30 minutes or in the oven for 40 minutes until golden and soft, then cool. Squeeze out the garlic and mix with the butter, then roll into 6 even-sized balls. Transfer to a greaseproof paper-lined tray and freeze until solid.

To make the sauce, heat the oil in a pan over a medium heat, add the garlic and cook for a minute. Pop in the tomato pulp and oregano, bring to the boil and reduce by half. Add the peppers and reduce by half again. Finish with the salt and sherry vinegar.

In a deep-sided saucepan, heat the oil to 170°C (340°F). Roll one-sixth of the risotto around a frozen butter ball. Coat in the flour, egg and then the breadcrumbs. Reshape into a ball and repeat with the remaining butter balls, risotto, flour, egg and breadcrumbs. Fry in batches for 5–6 minutes, then drain on kitchen paper.

Spoon the sauce onto plates, top with a squid ball and some crème fraîche.

# LANGOUSTINES WITH PISTO AND CURED TUNA AND TOMATO

## Serves 2

6 langoustines

10 red prawns

### For the pisto

150ml olive oil

1 aubergine, finely diced

1 red pepper, cored, deseeded and finely diced

1 green pepper, cored, deseeded and finely diced

1 onion, finely diced

3 garlic cloves, crushed

1 dried chilli, deseeded

2 large tomatoes

1 teaspoon sea salt

### For the tuna

4 tablespoons cooked tomato (see method)

6 slices of cured tuna

pinch of salt

15ml olive oil

**Pisto is originally from the regions of Murcia, Castilla-La Mancha and Extremadura. Essentially a Spanish ratatouille, it is made with tomatoes, onions, green and red peppers, aubergine or courgettes and olive oil. Here it is served to complement simple BBQ langoustines and red prawns, and cured tuna.**

If you want to use a BBQ, heat a BBQ until hot and the coals are white.

To make the pisto, heat a paella pan over a medium heat, then pour in a quarter of the oil. Add the aubergine and fry for 3–4 minutes. Remove and drain on kitchen paper.

Add a third of the remaining oil to the pan over a medium heat, then add the peppers and cook for 2–3 minutes. Drain on kitchen paper.

Add half the remaining oil, then fry the onion for 2–3 minutes and drain on kitchen paper. Finally, add the last of the oil and fry the garlic and dried chilli for 1 minute.

Grate the tomatoes through a sieve using a box grater, then add the pulp and juice to the oil with the garlic and chilli and fry for 5 minutes to reduce. Remove 4 tablespoons into a bowl, then pop all the fried vegetables back into the pan and give it a big stir. Warm through and season with the salt.

Place the langoustines onto the BBQ and cook for 1–2 minutes until charred. Then do the same with the prawns. Alternatively, you can use a griddle pan on the hob.

To serve, spoon the pisto onto plates and sit the seafood alongside. For the tuna, spoon the reserved tomato sauce onto a plate, top with the tuna, season with salt and drizzle over the olive oil.

# VIGO SEAFOOD FLATBREAD

**Serves 6**

---

500g strong white bread flour, plus extra for dusting

75ml olive oil

7g dried instant yeast

warm water, to bring the dough together

### For the sauce

50ml olive oil

300g tomato pulp

3 garlic cloves, crushed

pinch of pimentón ahumado (smoked paprika)

pinch of salt

### For the topping

200g clams, cleaned

splash of white wine

50ml olive oil

200g Tetilla cheese, sliced

4 octopus tentacles, cooked

8 baby squid, cleaned

pinch of pimentón ahumado (smoked paprika)

**Vigo is Galicia's fishing city – you've probably eaten fish from the port of Vigo dozens of times and the largest quantity of fresh fish in Europe enters the port here. This recipe uses Vigo's most popular produce to crown a cheesy, tomatoey flatbread.**

If using a BBQ, heat a BBQ until hot and the coals are white. Preheat the oven to 200°C (180°C fan)/400°F/gas 6 or heat a pizza oven to 400°C (750°F).

In a large bowl, mix the flour, 50ml of the olive oil and yeast together with enough warm water to make a soft dough. Knead together for 2 minutes, then cover and leave to prove at room temperature for 10 minutes.

Meanwhile, put all the ingredients for the sauce in a pan and bring to the boil. Reduce by half, then remove from the heat and leave to cool.

In a medium saucepan with a lid over a high heat, cook the clams in the white wine for 3–4 minutes until fully opened. Discard any that haven't fully opened. Add the clam cooking liquor to the tomato sauce.

Oil a large paella pan with 25ml of the olive oil, then roll out the dough on a floured work surface so it's the same size as your pan. Top with the cheese, drizzle with another 25ml olive oil, then bake in the oven for 12–15 minutes, or the pizza oven for 8–10 minutes.

Brush the octopus and squid with the remaining 25ml oil and the pimentón. Grill the octopus on the BBQ for 4 minutes and the squid for 2 minutes. Alternatively, you can cook them in a griddle or frying pan on the hob.

Spoon the tomato sauce over the cheesy flatbread and top with the cooked clams, squid and octopus.

# GARLIC BUTTER LOBSTER WITH ZARANGOLLO

**Serves 4**

150g butter, softened

zest of 1 lemon

1 garlic bulb, roasted and flesh
    squeezed out (see page 28)

small bunch of flat-leaf parsley,
    chopped

2 lobsters, cut in half lengthways

100ml olive oil, plus extra
    for drizzling

2 courgettes, sliced

2 onions, diced

6 eggs

pinch of chilli flakes

sea salt

Cieza olives, to serve

**The most important ingredient in Murcian cuisine is the vegetable. Vegetables are found in nearly every recipe and zarangollo is a common dish of scrambled eggs with courgette, onion and occasionally potatoes. Here I've served it on the side of lobster smothered in a delicious garlic butter.**

Preheat the oven to 200°C (180°C fan)/400°F/gas 6 or heat a pizza oven to 400°C (750°F).

Mix together the butter, lemon zest, roast garlic, parsley and a pinch of salt. Sit the lobsters in a paella pan, dot with the butter, then pop in the oven for 15 minutes, or the pizza oven for 6–8 minutes.

To make the zarangollo, heat another paella pan over a medium heat, add the oil, then fry the courgettes and onions for 3–4 minutes until softened. Season with a pinch of salt, then whisk in the eggs and give it all a big stir. Gently cook and keep stirring for 5 minutes until the eggs are just cooked. Sprinkle over the chilli flakes and drizzle with olive oil. Serve with the lobsters and olives.

# VALENCIA BEANS AND RED PRAWNS

**Serves 2**

---

75ml olive oil, plus extra for drizzling

2 garlic cloves, chopped

1 onion, diced

¼ leek, diced

½ carrot, peeled and diced

¼ green pepper, cored, deseeded
    and diced

3 bay leaves

2 whole smoked chilli peppers
    (or a pinch of chilli flakes)

300g cooked butter beans

splash of white wine

small bunch of flat-leaf parsley,
    chopped

8 red prawns, split lengthways

sea salt

**Located on the east coast, the 2,000-year-old city of Valencia boasts wide sandy beaches, striking architecture, a buzzing food scene and culture. It has its own language (a dialect of Catalan) and unique cuisine, with a focus on rice, seafood and meat. This dish showcases red prawns on a bed of white beans and vegetables.**

If you want to use a BBQ, heat a BBQ until hot and the coals are white.

Heat a medium paella pan and, when hot, add the oil, then add the garlic, all the vegetables, the bay leaves and the smoked peppers. Cook for 2–3 minutes, then stir in the beans, 50ml water and the wine and cook for 3–4 minutes. Season with salt and finish with the parsley.

Meanwhile, pop the prawns onto the BBQ, drizzle with oil and season with salt, then cook for 2–3 minutes until charred, turning once or twice. Alternatively, grill on high for 3–4 minutes.

To serve, remove the smoked peppers (if using) from the beans and then pile the prawns on top of the beans and drizzle with extra olive oil if desired.

# WHITE BEANS WITH LARDO AND CLAMS

**Serves 4**

---

50ml olive oil, plus extra to serve

100g lardo, sliced

100g Serrano ham, sliced

4 garlic cloves, crushed

1 large spring onion, chopped

2 smoked dried chilli peppers, deseeded

100g tomato pulp

250g *alubias blancas* (white beans, such as cannellini), soaked overnight and drained

300ml red wine

750ml fish stock

3 bay leaves

400g clams, cleaned

**Clams and white beans are a classic combination originating from Asturias. I've also added lardo and Serrano ham, a slow-aged ham made from a hind pork leg cut. Serrano ham is made from the more common white pig and the secret to its flavour lies within its delicate ageing process and the addition of a simple ingredient – sea salt.**

Heat a BBQ until hot and the coals are white. Alternatively, you can cook this on the hob.

Heat a large paella pan until hot, drizzle in the oil, then fry the lardo and ham for 2–3 minutes to render down the fat. Add the garlic, spring onion and smoked peppers and cook for 2 minutes. Then add the tomato pulp, drained beans, red wine, three-quarters of the stock and the bay leaves and bring to the boil. Reduce the heat and simmer for 20 minutes.

When the beans are almost cooked, add the clams and the remaining stock, give it all a big stir and cook for another 5 minutes until the clams are all fully opened.

Discard any clams that haven't opened, drizzle with olive oil and serve.

# BLACK RICE WITH SQUID, MONKFISH AND OCTOPUS

**Serves 8**

75ml olive oil

3 garlic cloves, crushed

1 onion, diced

400g tartana paella rice

3 bay leaves

1.2 litres hot chicken stock

pinch of saffron

1 teaspoon pimentón ahumado
    (smoked paprika)

2 tablespoons squid ink

a few sprigs of oregano, leaves picked

5 large sun-blush tomatoes sliced

juice of ½ lemon

a few sprigs of flat-leaf parsley,
    chopped

sea salt

### For the fish

50ml olive oil

juice of ½ lemon

pinch of pimentón ahumado
    (smoked paprika)

a few sprigs of oregano, leaves picked

1 monkfish, tail membrane removed

3 octopus tentacles, cooked

2 squid, cleaned

**This dish is based on the classic arroz negro, also known as black rice, a traditional Spanish dish hailing from the coastal regions of Valencia and Catalonia. It is cooked using a paella pan and squid ink, which gives it its characteristic black colour as well as a spectacular flavour.**

Heat a BBQ until hot and the coals are white.

Heat a large paella pan on the BBQ and pour in the olive oil. When hot, add the garlic and onion and cook for a minute, then stir through the rice and bay leaves and coat all over with the oil. Add three-quarters of the stock, bring to a bubble, then pop in the saffron, pimentón, squid ink, oregano and tomatoes, give it a big stir, then simmer for 15 minutes.

Pour the olive oil for the fish onto a tray, then mix in the lemon juice, pimentón and oregano. Roll the monkfish, octopus and squid in the flavoured oil. Skewer up the fish on different skewers, then place the monkfish skewers onto the BBQ and cook for 6–8 minutes. Pop the octopus skewers on and cook for 4–5 minutes. Finally, add the squid skewers and cook for 2–3 minutes, turning and brushing over the leftover flavoured oil occasionally.

Pop the fish onto a board and slice.

Make sure the rice is hot and bubbling, then finish with the remaining stock. Stir through the sliced fish, squeeze over the rest of the lemon, season with salt and sprinkle over the parsley to serve.

# BBQ FISH WITH PADRÓN PEPPERS AND MOJO SAUCE

**Serves 6–8**

12 padrón peppers

2 large mackerel, gutted

1 garlic clove, crushed

50ml white wine vinegar

250ml olive oil

6 small monkfish tails

2 Megrim sole, heads removed

6 sardines

5 anchovies

### For the mojo sauce

4 slices of baguette, diced

100ml olive oil

3 garlic cloves

small bunch of flat-leaf parsley or coriander

1 teaspoon cumin seeds

3 tablespoons sherry vinegar

sea salt

**This fresh and vibrant green mojo sauce originates from the Spanish Canary Islands and is usually made with olive oil, garlic, coriander and vinegar. Here I've used it to top a variety of simple BBQ fish, but it's also great with chicken and vegetables.**

Heat a BBQ until hot and the coals are white.

To make the sauce, fry the baguette in a drizzle of the olive oil until crisp, then drain and leave to cool. Crush the garlic to a paste with a pinch of salt, then chop with the flat-leaf parsley or coriander, cumin seeds and croutons until quite fine. Add the sherry vinegar and remaining oil and mix well.

Fry the padrón peppers in the baguette pan for 5 minutes until crisp and slightly charred. Season with salt.

Place the mackerel into a BBQ fish rack and mix the garlic, white wine vinegar and olive oil in a spray bottle. Place the mackerel on the BBQ, spray the oil mixture over the fish and cook for 2–3 minutes. Flip over, spray again and cook for a further 2–3 minutes. Then pop the mackerel onto a warm tray and set aside.

Fill the fish rack with the monkfish and sole, spray with the oil and pop on the BBQ. Cook for 2–3 minutes, flip over, spray again and cook for a further 2 minutes. Transfer to the tray with the mackerel.

Finally, fill the rack with the sardines and anchovies, pop on the BBQ, spray with oil and cook for 1–2 minutes. Flip over, spray again and cook for 1 minute.

To serve, pile the fish onto a platter, then top with padrón peppers and mojo sauce.

# SEVILLE ESCABECHE MACKEREL

## Serves 2

2 mackerel, gutted, heads and
    backbones removed

2 Seville oranges, sliced

3 bay leaves

mixture of 1 part white wine
    vinegar and 5 parts olive oil,
    in a spray bottle

1 purple spring onion, sliced, to serve

### For the sauce

2 large tomatoes

1 small garlic clove

15ml sherry vinegar

50ml olive oil

6 pink peppercorns, crushed

2 star anise

1 bay leaf

a few sprigs of thyme, chopped

pinch of pimentón ahumado
    (smoked paprika)

pinch of sea salt

1 small green pepper, cored,
    deseeded and diced

**Escabeche is a dish found throughout Spain, Portugal and Latin America. It generally means a dish of marinated fish, meat or vegetables, usually cooked or pickled with vinegar and then flavoured with citrus and spices. It works beautifully with super-fresh mackerel.**

If you want to cook this on the BBQ, heat a BBQ until hot and the coals are white.

To make the sauce, grate the tomatoes over a sieve and bowl with a box grater, pop the pulp into a larger bowl, then grate in the garlic. Add the remaining sauce ingredients and give it a big stir.

Place the mackerel onto a BBQ fish rack and sit the orange slices and bay leaves around the fish. Clip shut, then spray with about 1 tablespoon of the vinegar and oil mixture. Sit the rack on the BBQ and grill the fish for 2–3 minutes on each side. Alternatively, grill in the oven for 3 minutes, then flip over and cook on the other side for 3 minutes. Remove from the heat and place on a tray.

To serve, spoon two-thirds of the sauce onto a platter, top with the mackerel and oranges, spoon more sauce over the top, then sprinkle over the spring onion. Leave to marinate for 15 minutes or eat straight away.

# HAKE PIL PIL

**Serves 4**

---

400g hake fillet, cut into 4 small
    fillets
1 tablespoon fine salt
100g plain flour, seasoned
2 eggs, beaten
olive oil, for frying

**For the aioli**
3 egg yolks
1 tablespoon Dijon mustard
200ml olive oil
1 garlic clove, crushed to a paste
    with a pinch of salt
1 tablespoon red pepper paste
sea salt and freshly ground black
    pepper

**To serve**
chopped flat-leaf parsley
lemon wedges

**This dish combines Basque hake with a pimento pepper mayonnaise, the perfect pairing for fried fish. Serve sprinkled with parsley and lots of lemon wedges alongside for squeezing over the top.**

To make the aioli, whisk the egg yolks and Dijon mustard together in a bowl, then slowly add the oil, whisking continuously until thickened. Add the garlic and red pepper paste, give it a good mix and season.

Salt the fresh hake for 10 minutes, then wash and pat dry with kitchen paper. Cut the hake fillets into 1cm-thick strips, then coat in the seasoned flour, then the egg.

Pour enough oil into a frying pan until it is 8cm deep and heat to 180°C (350°F). Shallow-fry the hake for 1 minute on each side until crisp and golden.

To serve, pile the hake onto a platter and dot with the aioli. Sprinkle over the parsley and serve with the lemon wedges alongside for squeezing.

# BBQ MULLET WITH RED PEPPER AND ANCHOVY STEW

**Serves 4**

---

50ml olive oil

1 onion, diced

2 garlic cloves, chopped

1 red pepper, cored, deseeded and diced

4 teaspoons red pepper paste

400g fresh tomatoes, chopped

2 medium potatoes, peeled and diced

5 bay leaves

250ml white wine

2 red mullet, gutted

2 slices of lemon

1 teaspoon Espelette pepper and salt, mixed

8 large fresh anchovies, backbones removed

**I whipped up this fisherman's stew using the fantastic fresh anchovies and red mullet that I bought at the incredible Mercado San Martín market in San Sebastián. Top-quality fish like this just needs a few vegetables, some garlic, oil and wine and you've got yourself and some lucky guests an amazing meal.**

Heat a BBQ until hot and the coals are white.

To make the stew, pop the olive oil into a large frying pan over a medium heat, then add the onion, garlic, pepper, pepper paste, tomatoes, potatoes, three of the bay leaves and the wine and give it all a big stir. Gently simmer for 10–15 minutes until the potatoes are cooked.

Fill the cavity of each red mullet with a slice of lemon and a bay leaf, place onto a skewer and cook over the coals on the BBQ for 8–10 minutes, turning occasionally.

Add the Espelette pepper and salt mix to the stew, give it a big stir, then pop the anchovies in and cook over a medium heat for a further 2 minutes.

To serve, spoon the stew onto a platter and sit the red mullet on top.

# ASTURIAS SARDINES

**Serves 2**

4 padrón peppers

50ml olive oil

8 fresh sardines, backbones removed

150g tin of sardines, oil reserved

juice of ½ lemon

handful of frisée and lollo rosso
leaves

1 spring onion, sliced

sea salt and freshly ground black
pepper

**Asturias is full of mountainous landscapes, rugged coastlines, even brown bears! Here I'm using one of its finest coastal products: sardines. But it's not just fresh sardines, as I've made a sort of sardine sandwich of two fresh sardines filled with top-quality tinned sardines and a padrón pepper. A very Spanish fish sandwich!**

Fry the padrón peppers in half the olive oil and a pinch of salt for 3–4 minutes, then pop into a bowl and leave to cool. When cool, remove the stalks.

Lay the sardines skin-side down, then top four sardines with a padrón pepper each and a spoonful of tinned sardines. Season with salt, then lay another sardine on top, skin-side up. Press down slightly. Fry the sardines in a hot pan with the remaining olive oil until the skin is crispy, then flip over and cook the other side. They shouldn't take longer than 2–3 minutes in total.

To make the dressing, whisk together the oil from the tinned sardines, the lemon juice and the olive oil from the frying pan. Season well.

To serve, sit the sardines on a plate, alongside the salad leaves and spring onion, then spoon over the dressing.

# BAKED HAKE AND CLAMS WITH WHITE ASPARAGUS

## Serves 6

100ml olive oil

2 large spring onions, halved lengthways

2 garlic cloves, crushed

6 large tomatoes, cut into chunks

3 bay leaves

1 lemon, halved

800g hake fillet

300g clams

12 white asparagus spears

sea salt

### For the salsa verde

2 tablespoons sherry vinegar

1 tablespoon Dijon mustard

small bunch of coriander, chopped

small bunch of mint, chopped

small bunch of flat-leaf parsley, chopped

2 tablespoons capers

juice of 1 lemon

50ml olive oil

**This dish is a fantastic combination of fish and seafood, cooked with just a handful of fresh ingredients to really let their flavour shine. Serve simply with some white asparagus, all drizzled with a fresh super-herby salsa verde to take it to the next level.**

Heat a BBQ until hot and the coals are white. Preheat the oven to 200°C (180°C fan)/400°F/gas 6 or heat a pizza oven to 400°C (750°F).

For the salsa verde, pound all the ingredients together in a pestle and mortar to make a coarse paste.

Heat a large ovenproof dish on the BBQ or the hob, pour in half the oil, then add the spring onions and cook for 2–3 minutes until charred. Pop in the garlic, tomatoes, bay leaves and a splash of water and bring to the boil. Add the lemon, sit the hake on top and drizzle with the remaining oil. Season with salt, then roast in the oven for 15–20 minutes or in the pizza oven for 10 minutes. Pop in the clams and continue to roast for another 5 minutes.

Meanwhile, peel the asparagus bases with a potato peeler and place into boiling salted water for 6 minutes. Drain, then pop onto a plate. Dot with half the salsa verde and a drizzle of olive oil if desired.

Dot the remaining salsa verde over the hake to serve.

# JOSÉ'S TUNA TWO WAYS

## TUNA WITH ONIONS Serves 4

2 large onions, sliced
50ml olive oil
2 garlic cloves, sliced
1 teaspoon dried oregano
50ml sherry
500ml hot fish stock
400g tuna steak, cut into large chunks
sea salt

**To serve**
1 onion, sliced
2 tomatoes, sliced
olive oil, for drizzling

**Who better to show me the seafood delights on offer at the Central Market in Cádiz than my good friend and top chef José Pizarro? The market has 54 stalls selling fish, crustaceans and molluscs, so we couldn't possibly come away without some fantastic produce to try. This is José's tuna steak recipe, cooked with caramelised onions and served with sliced fresh onion and tomato.**

Pop the onions and oil into a large casserole dish and cook over a low heat for 10 minutes until caramelised. Add the garlic and oregano, stir through, then pour in the sherry. Bring to the boil, then ladle in the hot fish stock and bring to the boil again. Cook until almost all the liquid has gone, then pop in the tuna and cook for 5 minutes.

Season with salt and serve with the sliced onion and tomatoes, drizzled with olive oil, alongside.

# TUNA TARTARE WITH PORK Serves 4

1 Ibérico pork bloomer
    (similar to bavette steak)
pinch of salt
50ml olive oil
15ml sherry vinegar
1 teaspoon capers
zest of 1 lemon
100g tuna belly, finely diced
20g dried tuna, diced
20g Ibérico ham, diced
caviar, to serve

**This dish from José uses two types of tuna – tuna belly and dried tuna – alongside two types of Ibérico pork, the world-famous ham and the less well-known pork bloomer, a cut which is similar to a bavette steak.**

Heat a BBQ until hot and the coals are white.

Sprinkle the Ibérico pork bloomer all over with the salt, then pop onto the BBQ and cook for 2 minutes on each side. Alternatively, you can cook the pork in a frying pan on the hob. Remove the pork from the heat and leave to rest for 5 minutes. Then dice finely.

Mix the olive oil, vinegar, capers and lemon zest with the diced pork, tuna belly, dried tuna and Ibérico ham. Spoon onto plates, then top with caviar to serve.

# JOHN DORY WITH TOMATO SEAFOOD STEW

**Serves 6**

---

2 very large tomatoes

100ml olive oil

3 garlic cloves, crushed

pinch of pimentón ahumado
   (smoked paprika)

1 sprig of rosemary, leaves picked

25ml sherry

1.5kg John Dory, gutted

1 lime, sliced

½ onion, sliced

a few sprigs of flat-leaf parsley

spray of 1 part white wine vinegar
   and 5 parts olive oil

3 large langoustines

200g clams, cleaned

8 large red prawns, shell on

8 medium prawns, shell on

**Another fish and seafood spectacular! An array of different-sized prawns and clams are served crowned with a John Dory, stuffed with lime, onion and parsley to pack it full of flavour. The delicate but meaty flesh of the fish goes so well with the tomatoey seafood stew.**

Heat a BBQ until hot and the coals are white or preheat the oven to 200°C (180°C fan)/400°F/gas 6.

Start by making the sauce. Grate the tomatoes on a box grater over a sieve.

In a large paella pan over a medium heat, add the olive oil and garlic. Pour in the tomato pulp from the sieve along with the pimentón, rosemary and sherry. Bring to the boil, then reduce the heat and simmer for 5 minutes.

Place the John Dory onto a BBQ rack, dot with the lime slices and fill the cavity with the sliced onion and sprigs of parsley. Spray with the oil and vinegar mixture, then place the rack onto the BBQ and cook the fish for 3–4 minutes, spraying occasionally. Flip over and repeat, popping the langoustines on to cook for the last 2 minutes. Alternatively, cook in the oven for 15 minutes, turning halfway through.

Meanwhile, bring the sauce to the boil again, then pop in the clams and prawns and cook for 5 minutes until all the clams have opened (discard any that don't open).

To serve, spoon the sauce and shellfish onto a platter. Remove the John Dory from the rack and sit it on top.

# PUMPKIN AND TOMATO DORADA

## Serves 2

---

1 teaspoon cumin seeds

1 teaspoon coriander seeds

1 x 600g dorada, gutted, descaled and fins removed

100ml olive oil

1 bay leaf

1 lemon

a few sprigs of coriander, parsley and mint

300g pumpkin, cut into 2 x 2cm-thick slices

1 large tomato

1 garlic clove

50ml thick Greek yogurt

sea salt

**Dorada is a type of sea bream commonly found in Spain and sometimes called gilthead bream. Found in many Spanish restaurants because it's so tasty, here I've paired it with wedges of pumpkin, an easy fresh tomato sauce and a garlicky herby oil. Dollop with thick yogurt to serve as a wonderful contrast to the herb oil.**

Heat a BBQ until hot and the coals are white or preheat the oven to 200°C (180°C fan)/400°F/gas 6.

Pop the cumin and coriander seeds into a small pan and toast for a minute or two until they smell fragrant, then pop into a pestle and mortar and pound until coarse.

Marinate the dorada in 25ml of the oil with the bay leaf for 10 minutes. Then fill the cavity with two lemon slices, some of the herbs, and sprinkle a pinch of the spice mix into the cavity as well.

Season the fish with salt, then place onto a BBQ rack with a couple more lemon slices and the pumpkin. Drizzle over a little more oil, pop on the BBQ and cook for 6–8 minutes, turning halfway through cooking. Alternatively, cook on a roasting tray in the oven for 12–15 minutes.

Grate the tomato over a sieve with a box grater, pour the liquid over the fish, then mix the pulp with a splash of olive oil and the remaining spices, finishing with a squeeze of lemon juice.

To make the herb oil, chop the rest of the herbs, pop into the pestle and mortar with the garlic and pound to a paste. Then mix in a squeeze of lemon juice and the remaining oil.

To serve, remove the pumpkin from the rack. Lay on the serving plate, spoon over the tomato sauce, sit the fish on top and dot with the herb oil and yogurt.

# GIRONA ANCHOVY AND POTATO TART

**Serves 6**

---

4 large tomatoes

100ml olive oil

a few sprigs of oregano, leaves picked

3 large potatoes

2 garlic cloves, crushed

12 anchovies in oil

6 boquerones

6 green olives

6 black olives

a few leaves of flat-leaf parsley

a few sprigs of rock samphire

sea salt

**Anchovies (anxoves in Catalan) are salted in various places around the Gulf of Roses on the Catalan coast, although the place that's most renowned for the tradition is the city of L'Escala. The Greeks introduced the technique of conserving with salt, and the Romans later continued the system. You can buy the anchovies (called boquerones) with the salt removed and ready to add to salads, pasta or just served on bread. Here I've used them to top a potato and tomato tart.**

Grate the tomatoes through a sieve with a box grater, then pop into a pan with half the olive oil and oregano and bring to the boil. Reduce by half.

Peel and slice the potatoes very thinly with a mandoline.

Heat a large paella pan, add the remaining oil and the garlic, lay the potatoes all over the bottom to cover completely, then add another layer. Season with salt, sprinkle over the rest of the oregano and cook over a medium heat for 10 minutes until crisp.

To serve, top the potatoes with the tomato sauce and lay the anchovies and boquerones all over the potato. Scatter with the olives, parsley and rock samphire.

# CHARRED BROCCOLI WITH GRILLED LOCAL FISH

**Serves 6**

1 tablespoon sumac

6 green cardamom pods

1 teaspoon pimentón ahumado (smoked paprika)

1 teaspoon coriander seeds

1 teaspoon cumin seeds

1 teaspoon ground turmeric

1 teaspoon garlic salt

2 dorada salvajes, gutted, or 2 small sea bass, whole

1 corvina, gutted, or 1 large sea bream, cut into 4 steaks

1 lemon, sliced

mixture of 1 part white wine vinegar and 5 parts olive oil, in a spray bottle

2 heads of broccoli, broken into florets

75ml olive oil

75g almonds

a few sprigs of mint and flat-leaf parsley, chopped, to serve

### For the dressing

50ml olive oil

100g peanut butter of your choice (I used smooth)

zest and juice of 1 orange

1 tablespoon sherry vinegar

pinch of salt

**Corvina is often called white sea bass or speckled sea trout, but is actually a type of stone bass, and considered a delicacy in Spain and throughout southern Europe. If you can't get hold of any, then substitute with the best local fish you can find.**

Heat a BBQ until hot and the coals are white. Preheat the oven to 200°C (180°C fan)/400°F/gas 6 or heat a pizza oven to 400°C (750°F).

Pound the spices together in a pestle and mortar. Place the fish onto a BBQ rack and sprinkle with 2 tablespoons of the spice mix. Pop sliced lemon around the fish, then place onto the BBQ. Spray with the oil and vinegar mixture and cook for 4 minutes, spraying occasionally. Flip over and repeat on the other side. Alternatively, grill on high for 4 minutes.

Meanwhile, put the broccoli onto a roasting tray, drizzle in the oil and add 1 tablespoon of the spice mix. Pop in the almonds, give it all a big stir, then place into the oven or pizza oven and cook for 8–10 minutes until charred.

For the dressing, whisk together the olive oil, peanut butter, orange zest and juice, 1 tablespoon of the spice mix, the sherry vinegar and salt. Spoon the dressing over the cooked broccoli, sprinkle with the herbs and serve with the fish.

# PAN-FRIED COD, BABY SQUID AND ROMESCO SAUCE

**Serves 2**

For the romesco sauce

1 large red pepper, cored, deseeded
    and quartered

2 tomatoes, halved

1 slice of baguette, cubed

100ml olive oil, plus extra (optional),
    to serve

2 garlic cloves, crushed

50g hazelnuts

50g almonds

1 teaspoon pimentón ahumado
    (smoked paprika)

1 tablespoon sherry vinegar

sea salt

For the fish

75ml olive oil

1 dried nora pepper

a few sprigs of oregano

2 x 175g cod fillets, skin on

8 baby squid, cleaned

For the dressing

50ml olive oil

a few sprigs of flat-leaf parsley,
    chopped

1 teaspoon sherry vinegar

pinch of pimentón ahumado
    (smoked paprika)

squeeze of lemon juice

**Originating from Tarragona in Catalonia, romesco is a nutty, piquant and rich sauce made with roasted peppers and tomatoes, blended with nuts, garlic, olive oil and vinegar. In this recipe I've used both hazelnuts and almonds but you could use just one or the other, depending on what you have in your cupboards. Romesco was created by fishermen to be served with fish, so I've paired it with meaty cod fillets and some baby squid.**

If you want to use a BBQ, heat a BBQ until hot and the coals are white.

Place the pepper and tomatoes onto the BBQ rack and cook for 3–4 minutes until charred. Alternatively, you can char the pepper and tomatoes in a frying pan on the hob. Pop onto a tray to cool, then slice the pepper.

To make the romesco sauce, fry the bread in the oil for 2 minutes, then add the garlic and nuts and fry for 1 minute until just toasted. Place in a pestle and mortar with the pepper, tomatoes, pimentón and vinegar and pound until smooth. Season with salt.

Meanwhile, prepare the fish. Put half the oil into a pan and heat until hot. Add the nora pepper and oregano, then salt the cod and pop in the pan. Cook for 3–4 minutes, flip over and remove the pan from the heat. Cook the squid in another pan in the remaining oil over a high heat for 2 minutes. Mix together all the ingredients for the dressing, then pop the hot squid into it.

To serve, spoon the romesco sauce onto a plate, top with the cod, spoon over the squid and dressing and drizzle over more olive oil if desired.

# ANDALUSIAN TOMATO RICE AND FRIED FISH

**Serves 6**

2 large tomatoes

200g bomba rice

1 teaspoon pimentón ahumado (smoked paprika)

100ml olive oil

3 garlic cloves, crushed

25ml sherry

pinch of saffron

200g wood-roasted red peppers, sliced

2 bay leaves

sea salt and freshly ground black pepper

lemon wedges, to serve

### For the fish and seafood

500ml olive oil

150g plain flour, seasoned

5 small red mullet

8 anchovies

200g hake, skinned and sliced into 1cm pieces

1 large squid, cut into rings

**Bomba rice is a medium short-grain rice, perfect for this Andalusian recipe as it does not open up when cooked in lots of liquid, retaining a bit of bite for texture. This wonderful red rice dish perfectly complements an array of lightly battered fish and seafood, from meaty chunks of hake and red mullet to smaller anchovies and more delicate squid rings.**

Grate the tomatoes over a sieve with a box grater and chop all the skins into fine dice.

Mix the rice and pimentón together.

Heat the oil in a paella pan over a medium heat, pop in the garlic and cook for a minute. Then add the rice mixture and semi-fry for a minute to make sure all the rice is coated in the oil. Pour in the sherry, then all of the grated tomato, followed by the saffron, peppers, bay leaves and 250ml water and give it all a big stir. Gently simmer for 15–20 minutes, adding another 250ml water halfway through. Season, then leave to rest for 5 minutes.

To cook the fish, heat the olive oil to 180°C (350°F) in a deep-sided saucepan. Coat all the different fish in the seasoned flour and shake off any excess. Cook the fish in batches, starting with the red mullet for 2 minutes. Remove from the oil and drain on kitchen paper.

Then fry the anchovies for 1–2 minutes and drain. Make sure the oil has come back up to temperature and fry the hake for 2 minutes and drain. Finish with the squid, which will only take 1 minute.

To serve, spoon the rice onto plates and sit the fish and squid alongside with a wedge of lemon.

# TUNA WITH BUTTER GAZPACHO SAUCE

**Serves 2**

---

50ml olive oil, plus 1 tablespoon
   for drizzling

1 slice of baguette, cubed

2 tablespoons chopped flat-leaf
   parsley

½ tomato, diced

½ red onion, diced

1 tablespoon capers

1 green pepper, cored, deseeded
   and diced

6 black olives, stoned and sliced

½ garlic clove, diced

bunch of asparagus

2 x 200g tuna steaks

150g salted butter

juice of 1 lemon

50ml sherry

**You may be more familiar with Andalusian gazpacho as a bowl of chilled soup, but in this recipe I've combined the classic ingredients of a gazpacho with a nut brown butter to make a delicious sauce for some tuna steaks and charred asparagus. The tuna steaks just need the quickest of griddles, so this dish can be whipped up in no time at all.**

Heat a BBQ until hot and the coals are white, or you can also cook this dish on the hob.

Heat a medium frying pan over a high heat, pour in the oil, then add the bread cubes and cook for 2–3 minutes until golden and crisp. Transfer to a tray with the parsley, tomato, onion, capers, pepper, olives and garlic.

Place the asparagus spears onto the BBQ rack and char for 2–3 minutes or use a frying pan on the hob. At the same time, oil the tuna steaks with 1 tablespoon of olive oil, then griddle on all sides for 30 seconds–1 minute. Remove from the heat and leave to rest.

For the sauce, heat a medium pan until really hot, then spoon in the butter and cook for 1–2 minutes until nut brown. Squeeze in the lemon juice and pour in the sherry, then add the croutons and vegetables.

To serve, sit the asparagus onto plates, then slice the tuna and place alongside. Spoon over the sauce.

# ROASTED SEA BASS WITH TOMATOES AND OLIVES

**Serves 2**

---

1 x 700g whole sea bass, gutted
   and fins removed
1 lemon, sliced
a few flat-leaf parsley stalks
bunch of asparagus
25ml olive oil
pinch of salt

### For the sauce
150g tomato pulp
2 large tomatoes, cut into chunks
50ml olive oil
1 tablespoon sherry
100g olives of your choice, stoned

### For the dressing
1 tablespoon sherry vinegar
3 tablespoons tomato pulp
1 tablespoon chopped flat-leaf parsley
1 tablespoon sherry
1 garlic clove, crushed
50ml olive oil

**An impressive dish of whole sea bass, roasted on a bed of tomatoes and olives and drizzled in oil and sherry for extra Spanish flavour. I've complemented it with some grilled asparagus coated in a tomato and parsley dressing served alongside.**

If you want to use a BBQ, heat a BBQ until hot and the coals are white. Preheat the oven to 200°C (180°C fan)/400°F/gas 6 or heat a pizza oven to 400°C (750°F).

Start with the fish. Cut 3 or 4 deep slashes on each side, fill the cavity with the lemon slices and parsley stalks. Spoon the tomato pulp for the sauce into the base of a paella pan, sprinkle over the chopped tomatoes and sit the fish on top. Drizzle over the oil and sherry, then roast in the oven for 12–15 minutes, or in the pizza oven for 10 minutes, adding the olives for the last minute of cooking.

Whisk together all the ingredients for the dressing.

Pop the asparagus onto a tray, roll in the oil and season with the salt. Place onto the BBQ grill and char for 2–3 minutes, turning during cooking. Alternatively, you can cook in a griddle or frying pan on the hob.

Pop the asparagus onto a plate, spoon over the dressing and serve alongside the fish.

POULTRY
& GAME

# POUSSINS WITH CHARD AND LEMON BREADCRUMBS

**Serves 3**

150ml olive oil

400g new potatoes, sliced

1 garlic bulb, halved

1 green pepper, cored, deseeded
  and chopped

2 onions, cut into chunks

bunch of Swiss chard, stalks
  separated and chopped

4 eggs

3 poussins, spatchcocked

pinch of pimentón ahumado
  (smoked paprika)

sea salt

**To serve**

50g coarse breadcrumbs

15ml olive oil, plus extra (optional)
  for drizzling

zest of 1 lemon

splash of sherry vinegar

**Spatchcocked poussins are a great option for quicker cooking. Here I've served them alongside potatoes and scrambled eggs mixed with chard, scattered with zesty, crunchy lemon breadcrumbs and drizzled with sherry vinegar for true Spanish flavour.**

If you want to cook on the BBQ, heat a BBQ until hot and the coals are white. Preheat the oven to 200°C (180°C fan)/400°F/ gas 6 or heat a pizza oven to 400°C (750°F).

Heat a paella pan until hot, then add 100ml of the oil, the potatoes and garlic and fry for 3–4 minutes, stirring occasionally. Add the pepper and onions, give it all a big stir, then pop in the oven for 10 minutes until golden brown. Add the chard stalks and cook in the oven for 4 minutes, then pop onto the BBQ (or hob), stir through the chard leaves and the eggs and cook for 4 minutes.

Meanwhile, roll the poussins in the remaining 50ml oil, 1 teaspoon of salt and the pimentón, then put onto the BBQ rack and grill for 14–15 minutes, turning several times, until golden and cooked through. Alternatively, you can cook in a grill pan on the hob.

For the breadcrumbs, simply fry the breadcrumbs in the oil for 1–2 minutes until crisp and golden. Finish by stirring through the lemon zest.

To serve, sit the poussins on top of the potatoes, sprinkle over the lemon breadcrumbs and drizzle over the sherry vinegar and more olive oil if desired.

# MOROCCAN ORANGE CHICKEN

## Serves 4–6

---

100ml olive oil

1 large corn-fed chicken,
    cut into 8 pieces

1 tablespoon dried oregano

½ teaspoon cumin seeds

½ teaspoon ground turmeric

1 teaspoon coriander seeds

6 small red dried chillies

1 teaspoon pimentón ahumado
    (smoked paprika)

6 green cardamom pods

2 large spring onions, sliced

25g pistachios, shelled

50g almonds

50g pine nuts

3 star anise

1 cinnamon stick

6 large tomatoes, grated

200g dates, stoned

2 oranges, peeled and sliced

50ml honey

sea salt and freshly ground black
    pepper

**To serve**

a few sprigs of mint and coriander,
    chopped

1 pomegranate, seeds removed

**Although separated by the Alboran Sea, Morocco is one of Spain's closest neighbours, and so its cuisine has influenced and enhanced Spanish cooking. This chicken dish uses ingredients frequently featured in Moroccan recipes, such as cinnamon, nuts, dates and pomegranate seeds, alongside classic Spanish stars like orange and pimentón for a fantastic fusion of flavours.**

If you want to use a BBQ, heat a BBQ until hot and the coals are white. Alternatively, you can cook on the hob.

Heat a large paella pan and, when hot, drizzle in the oil, then fry the chicken portions for 5–6 minutes until deeply golden. You will need to do this in batches. Remove the chicken from the pan and place on a roasting tray.

Pound the oregano, cumin, turmeric, coriander seeds, dried chillies, pimentón and cardamom in a pestle and mortar until fine. Then, in the paella pan, fry the spring onions and nuts with the ground spice mix, star anise, cinnamon and tomato pulp for 2–3 minutes. Pop the chicken back in, along with the dates and oranges, then drizzle in the honey and cook for 20 minutes.

To serve, sprinkle over the herbs and pomegranate seeds and season.

# SEVILLE ORANGE MARMALADE DUCK SKEWERS AND CHICKEN WINGS

**Serves 2**

10 large chicken wings, skin on

2 large duck breasts, skinless and cut into 5cm cubes

50ml olive oil

juice of 1 orange

1 garlic clove, crushed

1 teaspoon sea salt

1 orange, cut into 8 pieces

1 large bunch of radishes

purple lettuce, to serve

### For the glaze

200g Seville orange marmalade

pinch of pimentón ahumado (smoked paprika)

pinch of cumin seeds

pinch of saffron

1 red chilli, sliced

1 green chilli, sliced

juice of 2 Seville oranges

**This recipe uses Seville's most famous culinary export: the bitter orange. Frequently used to make marmalade, in this recipe I've used both the marmalade and fresh orange to glaze and flavour BBQ chicken wings and duck skewers.**

Heat a BBQ until hot and the coals are white.

Marinate the chicken wings and duck cubes in the oil, orange juice, garlic and salt for 10 minutes.

Sit the marinated chicken wings on a BBQ rack and cook for 8–10 minutes, turning occasionally. Remove from the BBQ and set aside to rest.

On four metal skewers, skewer up the duck pieces, orange chunks and radishes. Cook on the BBQ for 4–5 minutes, turning occasionally. Remove from the BBQ and leave to rest.

To make the glaze, gently warm the marmalade, spices, chillies and orange juice in a pan over a low heat. Spoon half the glaze over the chicken wings and the duck skewers.

To serve, pile the chicken wings and duck skewers onto a platter, cut the lettuce into 4 pieces and sit on the side. Spoon over the remaining glaze and serve.

# CHICKEN WITH VERMOUTH AND PICADA

**Serves 4–6**

---

1.2kg chicken, cut into 8 pieces

75ml olive oil

3 garlic cloves, crushed

1 large potato, peeled and diced

1 tablespoon Dijon mustard

2 bay leaves

250ml white vermouth

300ml chicken stock

100ml double cream

3 long green peppers, cored, deseeded and sliced lengthways

sea salt and freshly ground black pepper

### For the picada

6 thin slices of baguette, cubed

75g almonds

50ml olive oil

2 garlic cloves

small bunch of flat-leaf parsley

**Vermouth is a fortified wine flavoured with various botanicals, such as seeds, herbs, spices and flowers. Served simply over ice or with a spritz of soda in Spain's numerous tapas bars, here I've combined it with double cream and chicken stock to cook a succulent chicken dish.**

In a large pan, fry the chicken in the oil over a medium heat for 5–6 minutes until golden brown all over. Season, then add the garlic, potato, mustard, bay leaves, vermouth and chicken stock. Bring to the boil, then pop in the cream and peppers and cook over a medium heat for 25–30 minutes.

For the picada, in a small frying pan over a medium heat, fry the bread and nuts in the oil until toasted. Transfer to a pestle and mortar and pound together with the garlic and parsley.

To serve, dot the chicken with the picada.

# PARTRIDGES WITH MEMBRILLO

**Serves 4**

6 purple artichokes

100ml olive oil

2 bay leaves

2 sprigs of thyme

2 sprigs of rosemary

2 garlic cloves, crushed

2 slices of lemon

pinch of salt

1 onion, sliced

1 tablespoon quince vinegar, to serve

### For the partridge

2 partridges, spatchcocked

50ml olive oil

squeeze of lemon juice

1 garlic clove, crushed

2 bay leaves

a few sprigs of rosemary

a few sprigs of thyme

### For the glaze

100g membrillo

2 tablespoons honey

25ml white wine

**This dish combines partridges with two popular Spanish ingredients: violet artichokes, grown throughout Valencia and Murcia, and membrillo, a sweet quince paste. Often served alongside Manchego cheese, here I've used this delicious paste to make a glaze for the partridges.**

Heat a BBQ until hot and the coals are white or preheat the oven to 200°C (180°C fan)/400°F/gas 6.

To prepare the artichokes, remove the lower outer leaves, peel the stalks with a peeler, then cut the top third off and discard. Cut into sixths. Put in a pan with the olive oil, bay leaves, thyme, rosemary, garlic, lemon slices and salt and cover with water. Bring to the boil and boil for 15 minutes, adding the onion after 10 minutes. Cook until nearly all the liquid has evaporated.

To make the glaze, pop all the ingredients in a pan, bring to the boil and stir.

Place the partridges onto a tray and press down. Cover in the oil, lemon juice, garlic and herbs, then roll around in the aromats. Pop onto the BBQ and cook for 5–6 minutes, turning occasionally and basting with the glaze. Remove from the BBQ and leave to rest for 5 minutes, continuing to baste with the glaze. Alternatively, you can cook the partridges in the oven for 12 minutes.

To serve, pile the artichoke mixture onto a serving plate, drizzle over the quince vinegar, then sit the partridges on top.

# SITGES CHICKEN AND WINE

## Serves 4–6

1.5kg chicken, cut into 8 pieces

150ml olive oil

8 thin slices of lardo

6 medium potatoes, peeled and sliced

pinch of cumin seeds

a few sprigs of rosemary

pinch of pimentón ahumado
    (smoked paprika)

100ml Catalonian wine

100ml sherry

3 garlic bulbs, halved

300g wild mushrooms, left whole

### To serve

100ml Catalonian wine

50ml olive oil

1 teaspoon pimentón ahumado
    (smoked paprika)

**The name Sitges comes from the Catalan word sitja, an underground storage space for grain. The town was constructed in the 11th century, built around Sitges Castle. In the 17th and 18th centuries, it became famous for the so-called 'Americans' who went off to trade with the Americas and eventually returned to show off their wealth by building extravagant summer houses. This recipe uses local Catalonian wine and pimentón to make a delicious sauce for the chicken, potatoes and wild mushrooms.**

If using a BBQ, heat a BBQ until hot and the coals are white. Preheat the oven to 200°C (180°C fan)/400°F/gas 6 or heat a pizza oven to 400°C (750°F).

Start by frying the chicken portions in a large paella pan in 50ml of the oil over a high heat for 4–5 minutes until deeply golden brown. Cover the chicken in the lardo, then pop in the oven for 25 minutes, or the pizza oven for 20 minutes.

In another pan, heat another 50ml of the oil and fry the potatoes, cumin seeds, rosemary and pimentón for 5 minutes until coloured. Add the wine and sherry and bring to the boil. Add the garlic bulbs, then transfer to the oven and roast for 25 minutes, or the pizza oven for 20 minutes.

Heat a pan over a high heat until very hot and sauté the mushrooms in the remaining 50ml oil for 2–3 minutes.

Pile the potatoes onto a platter, sit the chicken on top and spoon over the mushrooms. In the pan that you used to cook the mushrooms, heat the wine, oil and pimentón together until boiling. Remove from the heat and spoon all over the chicken, potatoes and mushrooms to serve.

# THE LOST VILLAGE CHICKEN AND MORELS

**Serves 6**

1 garlic bulb

150g butter, softened

a few sprigs of rosemary, needles removed

1 teaspoon pimentón ahumado (smoked paprika)

1.5kg chicken, spatchcocked and skin loosened

300g new potatoes

50ml olive oil

2 bay leaves

300ml chicken stock

3 large spring onions, sliced lengthways

100ml white wine

sea salt

### For the mushrooms

50g butter

1 garlic clove, crushed

200g fresh morel mushrooms, left whole

**El Acebuchal is known as the 'lost village' and is located between Frigiliana and Cómpeta in the mountains. Originally a resting place and meeting point for merchants who transported goods between the Costa del Sol and Granada, in 1949 General Franco sent the civil guard to close the village and empty it of its inhabitants, as he suspected they were hiding republican rebels. In 1998, Antonio García Sánchez, whose family previously lived in the village, decided to return with his wife. They rebuilt a few houses, opened an inn and started to revive the village.**

Preheat the oven to 200°C (180°C fan)/400°F/gas 6.

Make a paste with three garlic cloves and a pinch of salt and mix with the butter, rosemary and pimentón. Stuff the flavoured butter under the chicken skin and smooth it out so that it's all even.

Put the potatoes into a paella pan with the remaining garlic (halved), drizzle in the oil, add the bay leaves and sprinkle over some salt. Pour in the stock, sit the chicken on top and roast for 20 minutes. Remove from the oven, add the spring onions and wine to the potatoes and roast for a further 20 minutes.

For the mushrooms, heat a pan over a high heat, then pop in the butter. Once melted, add the garlic and mushrooms and cook for 3 minutes.

To serve, pile the potatoes and veg onto a platter, top with the chicken and spoon over the mushrooms and cooking juices.

# QUAIL WITH WHITE BEANS AND RIOJA

**Serves 4**

4 quails
25ml olive oil, plus extra (optional)
   to serve
sea salt and freshly ground black
   pepper

### For the beans

25ml olive oil
1 onion, finely diced
4 garlic cloves, crushed
300g jarred alubias blancas (white
   beans, such as cannellini)
150ml white Rioja
50ml double cream
2 bay leaves
50g butter
small bunch of flat-leaf parsley,
   chopped

**Rioja is world famous for its wine, but here I'm using the less well-known white Rioja, which makes up just 10% of the region's wine production. Combined with cream, white beans, garlic and herbs, it makes the perfect base for some simple roast quail. What better celebration of Rioja's most famous export?**

Heat the BBQ until hot and the coals are white or preheat the oven to 200°C (180°C fan)/400°F/gas 6.

Using scissors, cut through the backbone on both sides of the quails, turn them over and flatten down. Drizzle with the oil, season, then pop on the BBQ and cook for 5–6 minutes, turning halfway through cooking. Alternatively, cook in the oven for 10 minutes. Remove from the BBQ (or oven) and place onto a tray to rest.

For the beans, drizzle the oil into a pan over a medium heat, then add the onion and garlic and cook for 2–3 minutes until soft. Add the beans, wine, cream and bay leaves and bring to the boil, then reduce the heat and simmer for 3 minutes. Season, then stir through the butter and parsley.

To serve, spoon the beans onto plates and top with the quail. Drizzle with olive oil, if desired.

# BEEF FILLET WITH WILD MUSHROOMS

Serves 6–8

50ml olive oil

1kg fillet steak

1¼ teaspoons sea salt

4 large spring onions, sliced
    lengthways

25g butter

2 garlic cloves, crushed

500g wild mushrooms, left whole

a few sprigs of thyme, chopped

300g freshly podded peas

100ml chicken stock

2 tablespoons aged sherry vinegar

a few sprigs of flat-leaf parsley,
    chopped

**For the sauce**

50ml brandy

50ml sherry

100ml chicken stock

1 teaspoon sherry vinegar

**Beef and mushrooms is a classic combination and in this recipe I've paired meltingly tender slices of fillet steak with gorgeous wild mushrooms. This is a great dish to feed a crowd, so perfect for when you've got a few friends round for a BBQ.**

If you want to cook the steak on the BBQ, heat a BBQ until hot and the coals are white. Preheat the oven to 200°C (180°C fan)/400°F/gas 6 or heat a pizza oven to 400°C (750°F).

Drizzle half the oil all over the steak and sprinkle over 1 teaspoon of the salt. Cook on the BBQ rack for 2–3 minutes on each side until charred all over. At the same time, char the spring onions. Alternatively, you can cook both on the hob. Place the spring onions on a tray with the steak and then roast in the oven for 15 minutes or the pizza oven for 10 minutes. Remove and leave to rest, basting in the cooking juices.

For the mushrooms, heat a large paella pan over a medium heat, add the remaining oil, the butter and garlic. When smoking, pop in the mushrooms and cook for 2–3 minutes. Finish with the thyme, the remaining ¼ teaspoon of salt, the peas, chicken stock, sherry vinegar and parsley. Spoon onto a platter, slice the steak and sit it on top. Place the spring onions alongside.

Add the ingredients for the sauce to the steak pan, bring to the boil and reduce a little. Spoon over the steak to serve.

# TEARDROP PEA AND VEGETABLE SALAD WITH LAMB CHOPS AND POTATOES

**Serves 4**

200ml cider

50g butter

2 large potatoes, peeled and cubed into 1cm-thick pieces

1 sprig of rosemary

a drizzle of olive oil, plus extra (optional) to serve

8 lamb chops

sea salt and freshly ground black pepper

**For the salad**

3 cooked artichokes, sliced

150g teardrop peas (or garden peas if you can't find these)

150g fresh broad beans

100g fresh peas

3 spring onions, sliced

small bunch of flat-leaf parsley, chopped

3 sprigs of mint, leaves picked and chopped

100g soft goat's cheese

**For the dressing**

50ml cider

25ml cider vinegar

50g butter

25ml olive oil

**Basque cider is dry, not sweet, with no added sugar or gas. It is produced by mixing acidic, bitter and sweet apples and each cider house has their own preferred mixing methods. In this recipe I've used it not just to cook the potatoes but also for the salad dressing to coat the vegetables to complement the grilled lamb chops.**

If you want to BBQ the lamb chops, heat a BBQ until hot and the coals are white.

Pop the cider, butter, potatoes and rosemary into a pan, bring to the boil, then cook for about 10 minutes until the potatoes are soft and glazed. Coat the potatoes in the cider mixture while cooking.

Mix the vegetables and herbs for the salad in a large bowl.

Pop all the dressing ingredients into a pan, gently warm through, then stir in the goat's cheese. Pour over the salad while still warm. Season.

Oil and season the lamb chops, then place onto the BBQ and cook for 2–3 minutes until charred, turning once. Alternatively, you can cook the lamb in a griddle or frying pan on the hob.

To serve, spoon the salad onto a platter, top with the potatoes and lamb chops and drizzle over extra olive oil if desired.

# ROAST LAMB WITH CHICKPEA AND CHARD STEW

**Serves 6**

1 small leg of lamb, weighing about 1.2kg

50ml olive oil

pinch of salt

**For the stew**

1 large red pepper, cored and deseeded

200ml olive oil

2 onions, sliced

4 garlic cloves, crushed

6 large tomatoes, halved

50ml white wine

bunch of chard, stalks separated and sliced

a few sprigs of rosemary

pinch of pimentón ahumado (smoked paprika)

400g cooked chickpeas

sea salt

**A simple roast leg of lamb served alongside a chard and chickpea stew, making the most of the wonderful fresh produce Spain has to offer.**

If you want to cook on the BBQ, heat a BBQ until hot and the coals are white. Preheat the oven to 200°C (180°C fan)/400°F/gas 6 or heat a pizza oven to 300°C (570°F).

Place the lamb onto a roasting tray, drizzle in the oil, sprinkle over the salt and roast in the oven for 45 minutes, or in the pizza oven for 35–40 minutes. Remove from the oven and leave to rest for 15 minutes.

BBQ the pepper skin-side up for 2–3 minutes until charred, then flip over and cook the other side for 2–3 minutes. Alternatively, you can cook in a grill pan on the hob. Remove from the BBQ and slice.

Heat a large paella pan over a medium heat, pour in the oil, then cook the onions and garlic for 2–3 minutes. Pop in the tomatoes and wine and bring to the boil, then reduce the heat and simmer for 15 minutes. Pop in the sliced chard stalks, red pepper, rosemary and pimentón and bring to the boil. Stir through the chickpeas, season with salt and cook for 2 minutes. Then add the chard leaves, give it all a big stir and cook for 4–5 minutes until wilted.

Serve the stew with the sliced lamb.

# CHARRED VEGETABLES WITH PORK AND CHERRIES

**Serves 4**

---

1 red pepper, halved, cored and deseeded

1 green pepper, halved, cored and deseeded

1 yellow pepper, halved, cored and deseeded

1 bunch of asparagus

1 red onion, sliced

3 celery sticks, cut into thirds

1 courgette, sliced

3 pimento peppers, halved

100ml olive oil

sea salt

**For the pork**

2 pork fillets

zest and juice of ½ orange

25ml olive oil

a few sprigs of thyme

**For the sauce**

25ml olive oil

2 garlic cloves, chopped

zest and juice of ½ orange

a few sprigs of thyme, chopped

200g cherries, stoned

25ml sherry vinegar

1 tablespoon honey

a few sprigs of flat-leaf parsley, chopped

**This sweet cherry sauce provides a fantastic contrast to the charred vegetables. The pork is also marinated in orange juice for an extra touch of sweetness, and to give it a beautifully tender texture when grilled and sliced.**

If you want to use a BBQ for the vegetables and pork, heat a BBQ until hot and the coals are white.

Marinate the pork fillets in the orange zest and juice, oil, thyme and a pinch of salt for 5–10 minutes.

Coat all the vegetables in the oil and season with salt. Start by roasting the peppers on the BBQ for 4–5 minutes until charred. Alternatively, you can cook the veg using a grill pan on the hob or under a hot grill. Transfer the peppers to a tray.

Cook the asparagus for 2–3 minutes, then remove to the tray. Cook the onion and celery for 2 minutes and remove to the tray. Cook the courgette for 2–3 minutes until charred and remove to the tray. Finally, cook the pimento peppers for 2–3 minutes and add to the rest of the veg.

Pop the marinated pork on the BBQ and cook for 4 minutes on each side, then remove and leave to rest for 5 minutes. Alternatively, you can cook the pork in a grill pan on the hob.

To make the sauce, pop the oil into a large paella pan over a medium heat, then add the garlic, orange zest and thyme and cook for 1 minute. Then add the cherries, orange juice, vinegar and honey and bring to the boil. Reduce the heat and simmer for 2 minutes. Finish with the parsley and a pinch of salt.

To serve, slice the pork. Pile the vegetables onto plates and add the pork, then spoon over the cherry sauce.

# BRAISED OXTAIL

**Serves 4**

---

8 large oxtail pieces

25g plain flour, seasoned

50ml olive oil, plus extra to serve

1 onion, finely diced

1 celery stick, finely diced

3 carrots, finely diced

1 leek, finely diced

1 dried smoked red pepper, deseeded

300ml sherry

300ml chicken stock

3 large tomatoes, chopped

1 teaspoon salt

**Oxtail is traditionally a Córdoban stew, originating in the 16th century when it was created to take advantage of the tails of the bulls that came from the bullfights. Little by little, it became more popular and today it is a very traditional dish within Córdoban cuisine.**

Preheat the oven to 150°C (130°C fan)/300°F/gas 2.

Coat the oxtail in the seasoned flour, then fry in the olive oil in a large casserole pan over a high heat in batches for 5–6 minutes on each side until deeply coloured and browned. Transfer to a tray.

In the same pan that you cooked the oxtail, add all the vegetables, including the smoked pepper, and cook over a medium heat for 2–3 minutes until softened. Add the remaining ingredients, including the oxtail, and bring to the boil. Pop a lid on and cook in the oven for 6 hours.

To serve, sit the oxtail on a plate and spoon the sauce around. Drizzle with olive oil.

# SEVILLE PORK WITH PATATAS BRAVAS

**Serves 6**

---

2kg pork belly

a few sprigs of thyme, chopped

1 teaspoon salt

### For the potatoes

100ml olive oil

8 large potatoes, peeled and
    cut into sixths or eighths

4 garlic cloves, crushed skin on

3 bay leaves

1 teaspoon salt

### For the sauce

50ml olive oil

2 onions, diced

200g jarred roasted red peppers,
    blitzed

1 teaspoon pimentón ahumado
    (smoked paprika)

pinch of chilli flakes

1 teaspoon sugar

3 garlic cloves, chopped

**Translating as 'spicy potatoes', patatas bravas is
one of Spain's most famous dishes, often enjoyed
as part of a tapas spread. Here I've served it as a
side to a wonderful piece of roast pork belly with
crispy crackling.**

For the pork, score the skin in a diamond pattern, then mix
the thyme and salt together and rub into the skin. Pop the
pork into a roasting tin, skin-side up, and leave to marinate
for 1 hour.

Preheat the oven to 240°C (220°C fan)/475°F/gas 9.

Roast the pork in the oven for 30 minutes, then reduce the
temperature to 160°C (140°C fan)/325°F/gas 3 and cook for
a further 1½ hours.

For the potatoes, heat a paella pan and, when hot, pour in
the oil. Add the potatoes and fry for 5 minutes, then add the
garlic, bay leaves and salt. Roast in the oven for 30 minutes.

Meanwhile, make the sauce. Heat the olive oil in a pan over
a medium heat, add the onions and sweat for 2–3 minutes.
Then add the blitzed peppers, pimentón, chilli flakes, sugar
and garlic and bring to the boil. Reduce the heat and simmer
for 15–20 minutes.

To serve, slice the pork and spoon the sauce all over
the potatoes.

# SPICED ENTRECÔTE STEAK WITH BROAD BEANS AND ARTICHOKES

**Serves 2**

300g entrecôte steak

sea salt

**For the spice mix**

1 teaspoon cumin seeds

1 teaspoon coriander seeds

5 green cardamom pods

½ teaspoon ground turmeric

1 teaspoon dried marjoram

1 teaspoon sumac

1 teaspoon pimentón ahumado
   (smoked paprika)

**For the vegetables**

75ml olive oil

2 garlic cloves, crushed

1 small white courgette, diced

100g chorizo, halved lengthways
   and sliced

1 artichoke, prepped (see page 59)

200g broad beans

1 tablespoon spice mix (see above)

50g green olives

2 tablespoons chopped dill

**Entrecôte is a thin, boneless rib-eye steak, which makes it perfect for quick cooking on the BBQ. I've coated it with a delicious spice mix and served it alongside some beautiful green summer veg, mixed with a little chorizo for an extra Spanish flavour hit.**

Heat a BBQ until hot and the coals are white. Alternatively, you can also cook this dish on the hob.

Dry-fry the cumin and coriander seeds and cardamom pods in a frying pan for 1 minute, then pop into a pestle and mortar and pound until fine. Add the remaining spices and pound again.

Season the steak with 1 teaspoon of salt, then pop onto the BBQ and cook for 4 minutes, turning occasionally. Alternatively, you can cook in a frying pan over a high heat on the hob. Transfer the steak to a tray to rest, then sprinkle over 1 teaspoon of the spice mix and 25ml of the olive oil.

Pour the remaining 50ml olive oil into a paella pan over a medium heat, add the garlic and fry for 1 minute. Then add the courgette, chorizo and artichoke and cook for 1 minute. Pop in the broad beans, 150ml water and the spice mix and cook over a high heat for 3–4 minutes until all the liquid has been absorbed. Season with salt, then stir through the olives and dill.

To serve, spoon the vegetables onto plates and slice the steak and sit it alongside. Drizzle over the steak resting juices.

# CENA ESPAÑOLA DE JAMES

**Serves 4**

---

1kg potatoes, peeled and diced

1 litre olive oil

3 bay leaves

a few sprigs of rosemary

1 garlic bulb, halved

1 Ibérico pork bavette steak

1 Ibérico pork fillet, sliced into
    2cm-thick pieces

2 x 10cm centre-cut Ibérico pork ribs

12 Ibérico pork lizards (lagarto)
    (the strip of meat between the
    pork rib)

4 Ibérico pork chops

fine salt

### For the glaze

100ml Muscatel fortified wine

150g dark soft brown sugar

50ml sherry vinegar

**This dish showcases one of the most important components of Extremaduran cuisine: the Iberian pig. I've used five different cuts for my Spanish dinner here, all cooked simply on the BBQ and glazed with a sauce made with Muscatel and sherry vinegar, two other top Spanish ingredients.**

Heat a BBQ until hot and the coals are white.

Place the potatoes, oil, bay leaves, rosemary and garlic into a large, deep saucepan and cook gently for 20 minutes until the potatoes are just soft and slightly coloured.

To make the glaze, pop all the ingredients into a pan, bring to the boil, then simmer and reduce until just syrupy.

Season all the pork with salt. Start with the bavette steak and cook it on the BBQ for 2 minutes on each side. Remove from the BBQ and leave to rest.

Cook the fillet slices and centre ribs for 2–3 minutes, then flip over and repeat. Remove from the BBQ and leave to rest.

Pop the lizards on, cook for 1 minute on each side, then rest.

Finally, cook the pork chops for 2 minutes on each side, then set aside to rest.

To serve, use a slotted spoon to pile the potatoes, garlic and herbs onto a platter, roll all of the different pork cuts in the glaze, then sit them on top.

# VIGO PORK AND BEEF WITH TURNIP TOPS AND CHICKPEAS

## Serves 2

4 x 125g beef belly ribs

8 pork ribs, cut in half

1 large pork chop

### For the marinade

3 garlic cloves, chopped

1 teaspoon fine salt

small bunch of flat-leaf parsley, chopped

2 bay leaves

1 sprig of rosemary, leaves picked and chopped

1 teaspoon dried oregano

a few sprigs of thyme, leaves picked and chopped

150ml olive oil

### For the warm salad

2 garlic cloves, chopped

1 sprig of rosemary

1 bay leaf

50ml olive oil

bunch of turnip tops

200g cooked chickpeas

50ml white wine

**This hearty dish uses both beef and pork, which are coated in a garlicky herby marinade and then grilled. All that's needed on the side is some green turnip tops wilted with chickpeas. If you can't get hold of turnip tops, you can use kale or other similar greens instead.**

Heat a BBQ until hot and the coals are white or preheat the oven to 200°C (180°C fan)/400°F/gas 6.

Start by making the marinade. Pop the garlic and salt into a pestle and mortar and pound to a paste. Add all the herbs and pound again until you have a smooth paste. Mix in the olive oil until well combined.

Spoon a quarter of the marinade over the meat, then pop onto the BBQ and cook for 4–5 minutes, turning occasionally. Alternatively, griddle for 4–5 minutes until charred, then pop in the oven for 8–10 minutes. Remove from the BBQ (or oven) and leave to rest.

For the salad, in a medium frying pan over a medium heat, fry the garlic and herbs in the olive oil for 1 minute. Add the turnip tops and cook for 2 minutes until just wilted. Pop in the chickpeas and wine, season, then stir in a quarter of the marinade.

To serve, pile the salad onto plates, top with the meat and spoon the remaining marinade on top.

# SLOW-COOKED PORK WITH BELUGA LENTILS

## Serves 8–10

2kg pork loin off the bone, scored
1 teaspoon sea salt

**For the lentils**
75ml olive oil
2 small cooking chorizo
2 small black puddings
50g lardo
50g cooked pork shin
1 garlic bulb, halved
1 onion, peeled and cut into sixths
2 carrots, cut into chunks
2 celery sticks, cut into chunks
1 leek, diced
750ml chicken stock
splash of red wine
200g beluga (caviar) lentils
chopped flat-leaf parsley
1 tablespoon sherry vinegar
sea salt and freshly ground
    black pepper

**Beluga lentils cooked with pork shin, black pudding, chorizo and lardo beautifully complement this slow-roast pork.**

If you want to cook on the BBQ, heat a BBQ until hot and the coals are white. Preheat the oven to 240°C (220°C fan)/475°F/gas 9.

Place the pork in a large roasting tray, season with the salt and roast in the oven for 30 minutes. Reduce the oven temperature to 180°C (160°C fan)/350°F/gas 4 and cook for a further 2½ hours.

Heat the oil in a large pan over a medium heat, add the chorizo, black puddings, lardo and pork shin and cook for 2 minutes. Then add the garlic, onion, carrots, celery and leek and cook for 5 minutes. Next, add the chicken stock, red wine and caviar lentils and bring to the boil. Reduce the heat and simmer for 30 minutes. Sprinkle over the parsley, stir through the vinegar and season.

To serve, slice the pork, pop onto a plate and add a big spoonful of lentils.

# CASTILE BEANS AND MEATBALLS

## Serves 6–8

100g dried alubias de La Bañeza
(white beans)

1kg beef mince

small bunch of flat-leaf parsley,
chopped

3 garlic cloves, chopped

100ml olive oil

100g lardo, sliced

5 tomatoes, diced

1 onion, sliced

500ml passata

1 teaspoon dried oregano

300ml red wine

200g roasted red peppers in a jar,
sliced

sea salt and freshly ground black
pepper

**Castile and León is a region rich in pulses, and the largest producer in Spain. This recipe uses white beans from La Bañeza, which have a soft and buttery texture and hold their shape well when cooked, making them the perfect choice for a tomatoey stew to accompany beefy meatballs.**

Soak the beans in cold water overnight, then drain. Pop in a pan, cover with cold water, bring to the boil, then simmer for 1 hour. Drain and set aside.

Mix together the beef, half the parsley, 1 teaspoon of salt and one-third of the garlic. When evenly combined, shape into 12 large meatballs.

Heat a large pan over a medium–high heat until hot, then add half the oil and pop in the meatballs. Once the meatballs have coloured, turn them over, then add the lardo, rest of the garlic, the tomatoes, onion, passata, oregano and wine. Season, bring to the boil, then pop in the peppers and simmer for 15 minutes.

Add the beans and cook for a further 10 minutes, sprinkle over the remaining parsley, then drizzle over the remaining oil and serve.

# STEAK WITH STUFFED TOMATOES

**Serves 4**

---

1kg rib-eye steak on the bone

25ml olive oil

4 garlic cloves, diced

2 green peppers, halved, cored and deseeded

4 beef tomatoes

2 tablespoons pine nuts

200g cooked bomba rice

a few sprigs of flat-leaf parsley, chopped

sea salt

**To serve**

50ml olive oil

25ml sherry vinegar

**Make sure you get the biggest, juiciest beef tomatoes available so that you can pack them with as much of this tasty rice stuffing as possible. A great accompaniment to melt-in-the-mouth slices of rib-eye steak, all drizzled with the resting juices.**

If you want to cook this on the BBQ, heat a BBQ until hot and the coals are white. Preheat the oven to 200°C (180°C fan)/400°F/gas 6 or heat a pizza oven to 400°C (750°F).

Season the steak with ½ teaspoon of salt and the oil, then cook in a non-stick pan over a high heat for 3 minutes on each side. Place onto a tray with the garlic, then roast in the oven for 8–10 minutes, or in the pizza oven for 10 minutes. Remove from the oven and leave to rest.

Meanwhile, BBQ the peppers skin-side up for 3 minutes, then flip over and repeat on the other side. Alternatively, you can use a griddle or frying pan on the hob. Leave to cool a little, then chop into small pieces.

Cut the top fifth off the tomatoes and scoop out the flesh with a melon baller, being careful not to break the skin. Chop the centres of the tomatoes into small dice, pop into the steak pan and bring to the boil. Reduce by half, then add the peppers, pine nuts, cooked rice and parsley and season. Give it all a big stir, then fill the tomato shells full to the top with the rice mixture and sit the lids back on top. Place into an ovenproof dish and roast in the oven for 5 minutes until hot and bubbling. Spoon over the oil and vinegar to serve.

Slice the steak and serve with the tomatoes, spooning over the resting juices.

# VEAL CHOPS WITH MUSCATEL SAUCE

**Serves 4**

---

3 x 250g veal chops
50ml olive oil
1 large bunch of spring onions
sea salt

For the Muscatel sauce
50ml olive oil
2 onions, sliced
1 garlic bulb, halved
2 bay leaves
1 large potato, peeled and thinly
    sliced
25ml Muscatel fortified wine
50ml white wine
50g Muscatel raisins
100g chestnut mushrooms, sliced
100ml double cream

**Muscatel raisins are also known as Málaga raisins and are one of the region's most well-known culinary products. Made from sun-drying Muscat grapes, these raisins are said to have a unique quality, which is why they're enjoyed as raisins as well as being made into wine. In this recipe I've used both the raisins and wine to make a delicious sauce for coating veal chops.**

Heat a BBQ until hot and the coals are white or preheat the oven to 200°C (180°C fan)/400°F/gas 6.

Drizzle the veal chops with 25ml of the oil and season with 1 teaspoon of salt. Place onto the BBQ and cook for 6–8 minutes, turning occasionally. Alternatively, griddle for 2–3 minutes until charred, then pop in the oven for 8–10 minutes. Remove from the BBQ (or oven) and leave to rest for 5 minutes.

To make the sauce, in a large paella pan, heat the oil over a medium heat. Add the onions and cook for 8–10 minutes until slightly caramelised. Pop in the garlic, bay leaves, potato and Muscatel and bring to the boil. Then add 150ml water, the white wine, raisins, mushrooms and cream and bring to the boil again. Reduce the heat and simmer gently for 6–8 minutes.

Meanwhile, season the spring onions with a pinch of salt, drizzle with the remaining 25ml oil, then pop on the BBQ. Cook for 3–4 minutes until charred. Alternatively, cook in a grill pan on the hob.

To serve, spoon the Muscatel sauce onto plates, then pop a veal chop on the side with a pile of charred spring onions.

# CANNELLONI WITH BROAD BEANS AND LARDO

**Serves 6**

---

1 onion, halved

3 cloves

1 litre full-fat milk

1 bay leaf

75g butter

75g plain flour

grating of nutmeg

sea salt and freshly ground black
    pepper

### For the filling

1 teaspoon sea salt

1 teaspoon dried oregano

500g pork mince

500g beef mince

300g small cannelloni tubes

### For the beans

100g Serrano ham, cut into strips

100g lardo, cut into strips

50ml olive oil

2 garlic cloves, crushed

300g broad beans, podded

a few sprigs of flat-leaf parsley,
    chopped

**You might think of cannelloni as an Italian dish, but Catalan-style cannelloni are particularly popular in Barcelona and often enjoyed on Boxing Day, stuffed with the leftover meat from Christmas dinner. Here I've filled them with beef and pork mince and accompanied them with some broad beans flavoured with Spanish Serrano ham and lardo.**

If you want to use a BBQ, heat a BBQ until hot and the coals are white. Preheat the oven to 180°C (160°C fan)/350°F/gas 4 or heat a pizza oven to 300°C (570°F).

To make a classic béchamel, stud the onion with the cloves and heat the milk, onion and bay leaf until almost boiling. Reduce the heat and leave to simmer. Melt the butter in a medium saucepan over a medium heat, then add the flour and cook out for 1 minute. Slowly pour in the milk, whisking constantly until smooth. Season to taste, then add the nutmeg.

Mix the salt, oregano and pork and beef mince together until well mixed. Fill each cannelloni tube with the meat mixture until full and sit in a paella dish. Pour over the béchamel sauce, making sure all the cannelloni are covered. Bake in the oven for 30 minutes or the pizza oven for 20–30 minutes, until hot and bubbling and cooked through.

For the beans, in a small frying pan over a high heat, fry the Serrano ham and lardo in the oil for 3–4 minutes until crisp. Add the garlic, broad beans and a splash of water and cook over a high heat for 2 minutes until all the liquid has evaporated and the beans are warmed through. Sprinkle with the parsley and serve with the cannelloni.

# VERONICA'S STEAK, COURGETTE FLOWERS AND BBQ PEAS

### Serves 2

1 large sirloin steak on the bone
25ml olive oil
sea salt

### For the courgettes
1.5 litres vegetable oil, for frying
100g gluten-free self-raising flour
150ml dry cider
pinch of pimentón ahumado
    (smoked paprika)
pinch of salt
6 courgette flowers, stamen removed
squeeze of lemon juice

### For the peas
300g peas in the pod
50ml olive oil

**Here I've coated beautiful courgette flowers in a light Spanish-style batter using cider and pimentón. All you need to do with the peas is throw them straight on the BBQ, no need for podding, and serve up the veg alongside a piece of grilled sirloin – the perfect taste of Spanish summer.**

Heat a BBQ until hot and the coals are white. In a medium saucepan, heat the vegetable oil for frying to 190°C (375°F).

Drizzle the steak with the olive oil and season with 1 teaspoon of salt. Place onto the BBQ grill and cook for 3 minutes on each side. Remove from the BBQ and leave to rest.

Whisk together the flour, cider, pimentón and salt to make a light batter. Dip the courgette flowers into the batter and fry in batches for 2 minutes until crisp and golden. Drain on kitchen paper, then season with salt and squeeze over the lemon juice.

Place the peas into a metal sieve and BBQ in batches for 3–4 minutes until charred. Season with salt and drizzle with the oil.

To serve, place the steak onto a platter with a pile of peas and courgette flowers.

# TOLEDO CARCAMUSA

**Serves 4**

---

1kg beef shin, diced

50g plain flour, seasoned

50ml olive oil

2 onions, diced

2 celery sticks, diced

2 carrots, peeled and diced

1 garlic bulb, halved

200ml sherry

300g tomato pulp

a few sprigs of thyme, chopped

2 bay leaves

1 teaspoon sea salt

1 litre chicken stock

**To serve**

200ml chicken stock

500g cooked bomba rice

**Carcamusa is Toledo's most famous dish, made with slow-cooked pork loin, peas, tomatoes and white wine. There are many theories as to the origins of the name of the stew but most agree that it was created by José Ludeña and Rufo Herrera, who first served it in their restaurant Bar Ludeña before it was popularised and spread throughout Toledo.**

Coat the beef in the seasoned flour, then fry in the oil in an ovenproof dish over a high heat for 3–4 minutes until deeply coloured. You may need to do this in batches. Transfer the cooked beef to a roasting tray.

In the same pan, fry the onions, celery, carrots and garlic over a high heat for 2–3 minutes. Pour in the sherry, bring to the boil, then add the tomato pulp, browned beef, thyme, bay leaves and salt. Pour in the chicken stock and simmer for 5 hours over a low heat. Alternatively, you can cover and pop in the oven at 140°C (120°C fan)/275°F/gas 1.

To serve, heat the chicken stock and the cooked rice, season with salt and get it really hot. Serve a big spoonful of rice with the beef.

# PUDDING
# & CAKES

# ROSCOS FRITOS – DOUGHNUTS WITH STRAWBERRIES

**Makes 6**

3 tablespoons olive oil, plus 1.5 litres for deep-frying

2 star anise

1 egg

3 tablespoons caster sugar

2 teaspoons baking powder

1 tablespoon anise liqueur

3 tablespoons full-fat milk

zest of 1 lemon

200g plain flour, plus extra for dusting

**To coat**

100g caster sugar

1 teaspoon ground cinnamon

**To serve**

75g caster sugar

500g strawberries, quartered

**Roscos fritos (fried doughnuts) are Spanish-style doughnuts, with a different texture and slightly sweeter than the doughnuts you might be used to. They are a traditional Andalusian speciality often enjoyed around Holy Week, but they can also be served throughout the year.**

For the strawberries to serve, heat a non-stick frying pan over a medium heat and, when hot, add the sugar. Do not stir but carefully swirl in the pan until the sugar is brown and caramelised. This should take about 3–4 minutes. Once the sugar has caramelised, quickly stir through the strawberries. Remove from the heat.

In a medium saucepan, heat the deep-frying oil with the star anise to 170°C (340°F).

Mix all the remaining ingredients together for the doughnuts until the mixture resembles a soft dough. On a floured work surface, roll out the dough into six 10cm-long sausage shapes. Make a small hole at one end of each sausage, then poke the other end through to stick together and make a circle.

Mix together the caster sugar and cinnamon in a small bowl.

Fry the doughnuts in batches for 2–3 minutes on one side, then carefully flip over and cook on the other side for 2–3 minutes. Drain on kitchen paper, then coat in the cinnamon sugar and serve warm with the strawberries.

# CATALAN MIXED FRUITS WITH CAVA SABAYON

**Serves 2**

---

For the poaching liquid
juice of 1 orange
50ml cava
splash of brandy
75g caster sugar
2 star anise
1 cinnamon stick
1 vanilla pod, split
3 peaches, halved

For the sabayon
6 egg yolks
50g caster sugar
25ml cava

To serve
a few strawberries, blueberries
    and blackberries
1 níspero (loquat) or apricot, stoned
    and sliced
a few sprigs of mint

**Cava is perhaps Catalonia's most famous export, with the sparkling white wine enjoyed throughout Spain and across the world. The name cava comes from the Spanish word for 'cave', referring to the cellars where the wines age. Spanish sparkling wine was called champán or champaña until the 1970s when Spanish winemakers renamed their wine 'cava'. In this dessert, I've not only used it to poach the fruit but also to flavour the sabayon, a light sauce traditionally made with egg yolks, sugar and a sweet wine.**

If you want to BBQ the peaches, heat a BBQ until hot and the coals are white.

Start by making the poaching liquid. Half-fill a small pan with water, pop in all the ingredients and bring to the boil. Reduce the heat, then simmer for 5 minutes. Drain the peaches, then pop on the BBQ, flat-side down and cook for 3–4 minutes until just charred. Alternatively, you can cook the peaches in a frying pan on the hob.

To make the sabayon, sit a large glass bowl over the pan of poaching liquid over a medium heat. Add the eggs, sugar and cava to the bowl and whisk continuously until thick and at a ribbon stage.

To serve, pop all the fruits onto a platter and spoon over the sabayon. Blowtorch until just coloured, then dot with mint sprigs.

**Note:** If you do not have a cook's blowtorch, pop under a hot grill, making sure the platter is heatproof.

# LEÓN APPLE MEMBRILLO TART

**Serves 8–10**

---

**For the pastry**
625g plain flour, plus extra for dusting
1 tablespoon dried instant yeast
250ml warm water
120ml olive oil, plus extra for greasing
1 egg

**For the filling**
150g membrillo
3 apples, sliced

**For the glaze**
4 tablespoons honey
25ml olive oil

**This apple tart uses a layer of membrillo, the Spanish quince paste, underneath the thinly sliced apples. Drizzled with honey, it's simple and delicious.**

Place all the ingredients for the pastry into a stand mixer fitted with the dough hook attachment. Mix for 3 minutes, pop into a bowl and cover. If you don't have a mixer, then mix the ingredients together by hand and knead for 5 minutes. You can use this dough straight away or pop it in the fridge to chill overnight.

Preheat the oven to 240°C (220°C fan)/475°F/gas 9.

On a floured work surface, roll out the dough into a large rectangle. Grease and line a 30 x 40cm baking tray with baking paper. Pop the dough onto the tray and push it right up to the edges. Cover the dough with the membrillo, then lay the apple slices, overlapping, to cover the whole tart. Drizzle over half the honey and the olive oil and bake for 20–25 minutes.

Drizzle over the remaining honey while still warm, then slice and serve.

# SPICED SEVILLE ORANGES WITH CRÈME CARAMEL

**Serves 4**

For the caramel
150g caster sugar
squeeze of orange juice

For the filling
500ml full-fat milk
zest of 1 Seville orange
1 vanilla pod, seeds removed
3 large eggs, plus 2 egg yolks
100g caster sugar

For the orange
1 Seville orange, peeled
2 star anise
1 cinnamon stick
3 cloves
2 bay leaves
100g caster sugar
100ml water

**A pudding which makes the most of Seville's famous citrus export. The crème caramels are flavoured with orange as well as the vanilla and served alongside sticky caramelised slices of orange.**

Heat a non-stick frying pan over a medium heat and, when hot, add the sugar, 2 tablespoons of water and the orange juice. Do not stir but carefully swirl in the pan until the sugar is brown and caramelised. This should take about 3–4 minutes. Once the sugar has caramelised, spoon into four ramekins and set aside.

Preheat the oven to 130°C (110°C fan)/265°F/gas ¾.

Heat the milk, orange zest and the vanilla in a medium saucepan over a medium heat. In a bowl, whisk the eggs and sugar until combined. Pour over the warm milk mixture and whisk again. Then ladle the mixture onto the caramel. Place the ramekins into a bain-marie and bake for 45 minutes. Transfer to the fridge to chill overnight.

For the orange, pop all the ingredients into the caramel pan and bring to the boil. Remove from the heat and leave to cool and infuse. To turn the caramels out, loosen the edges with a sharp knife onto plates, then spoon the oranges on the side.

# RICE PUDDING WITH BAKED APPLES AND WALNUT BRITTLE

**Serves 6**

---

### For the rice
450ml full-fat milk
1 vanilla pod
100g caster sugar
1 small cinnamon stick
500ml double cream
75ml honey
150g bomba rice

### For the apples
100g marzipan
50g walnuts, chopped
4 large local apples, cored
100ml cider
1 cinnamon stick
3 star anise
4 tablespoons honey

### For the brittle
100g caster sugar
100g walnuts

**This is my own version of Spanish rice pudding, known as arroz con leche, which translates as 'rice with milk'. I've served mine with a walnut brittle, for a crunchy texture contrast, and walnut-and-marzipan-stuffed apples.**

If you want to cook on the BBQ, heat a BBQ until hot and the coals are white. Preheat the oven to 160°C (140°C fan)/325°F/ gas 3 or heat a pizza oven to 400°C (750°F).

For the brittle, heat a non-stick frying pan over a medium heat and, when hot, add the sugar. Do not stir but carefully swirl in the pan until the sugar is brown and caramelised. This should take about 3–4 minutes. Once the sugar has caramelised, stir through the walnuts, then carefully pour onto a non-stick mat or greaseproof paper and leave to set. Once set, break into shards.

In a paella pan, warm the milk and vanilla over a medium heat for 2 minutes. Add the sugar, cinnamon, double cream, honey and rice and stir through. Carefully transfer to the oven and bake for 20 minutes.

Meanwhile, mix the marzipan and chopped walnuts together. Stuff into the cored apples, then pop the apples, cider and spices into an ovenproof dish and bake in the oven for 30 minutes, or in the pizza oven for 10 minutes until the apples are just soft. Drizzle over the honey and bake for 2–3 minutes, then baste in all the juices.

Serve a big spoonful of rice pudding alongside the apples. Sprinkle over the walnut brittle.

# APRICOT AND BASIL CARNIVAL FLOWER

**Serves 6**

---

750ml sunflower oil, for frying

750ml olive oil, for frying

250g plain flour

150ml full-fat milk

250ml olive oil

6 eggs

7g sachet of dried yeast

To serve

12 apricots, stoned and halved

75ml apricot liqueur

a few sprigs of basil

icing sugar, for dusting

25g shelled pistachios

25g almonds

25g hazelnuts

**Around two-thirds of Spain's apricot production is located in Murcia. Apricots are mainly grown in the areas of Cieza, Abarán and Blanca, which produced 54,739 tonnes of the delicious fruit in 2021. In this recipe, I've poached the apricots in apricot liqueur and basil, and served them with a carnival flower sprinkled with nuts. You can buy the carnival flower moulds online, or bring one back from your next Spanish adventure.**

Pop the apricots and liqueur into a pan and cook over a medium heat for 5 minutes until just softened. Add the basil, then remove from the heat and leave to cool slightly.

Heat both the oils to 185°C (365°F) in a deep-sided saucepan, then pop the metal flower mould into the pan to heat up.

In a large bowl, whisk the flour, milk, olive oil, eggs and yeast together until lump free.

Carefully remove the flower mould from the hot oil, dip in the batter two-thirds of the way to the top, then plunge straight into the hot oil. Do not let it touch the bottom of the pan. After 20 seconds, start to jiggle the mould and, when golden in colour, the flower should release from the mould. With a slotted spoon, flip the flower over and cook for 2 minutes until evenly coloured. Remove from the oil with a slotted spoon onto a lined tray. Dust liberally with icing sugar.

To serve, spoon the apricot mix onto a plate, top with the flower and sprinkle with the nuts.

# CHOCOLATE AND CHERRY BEER CAKE

## Serves 8

---

butter, for greasing
6 eggs
175g caster sugar
125g plain flour
40g cocoa powder

**For the jam**
300g cherries, stoned
50ml cherry beer
100g caster sugar

**To decorate**
500ml whipped double cream
100g caster sugar
16 fresh cherries
cocoa powder, for dusting

**Spain's most well-known cherry-producing area is the Jerte Valley, located at the most northern part of the Extremaduran province of Cáceres, which produces over 200 different varieties of cherries. This cake uses not just cherries but also cherry beer for a super-flavourful jam filling, then is topped off with even more fresh cherries and a layer of whipped cream.**

Preheat the oven to 200°C (180°C fan)/400°F/gas 6. Grease and line a 22cm round cake tin with baking paper.

In a stand mixer, whisk the eggs and sugar to ribbon stage – when you move the whisk through the mixture it should leave a visible trail. Fold in the flour and cocoa powder, then pour into the prepared tin and level out. Bake for 45 minutes. Remove from the tin and transfer to a wire rack to cool. Split in half with a bread knife.

To make the jam, pop the cherries, cherry beer and sugar into a saucepan over a medium–high heat and bring to the boil. Reduce the heat and simmer for 15 minutes. Remove from the heat and leave to cool.

Spoon the jam all over the bottom layer of cake and sit the other layer of sponge on top. Spread the whipped cream all over the top.

Heat a non-stick frying pan over a medium heat and, when hot, add the remaining 100g sugar. Do not stir but carefully swirl in the pan until the sugar is brown and caramelised. This should take about 3–4 minutes. Once the sugar has caramelised, carefully dip in the cherries and pop onto greaseproof paper to cool.

Place the cherries on top of the cream and dust with cocoa powder to serve.

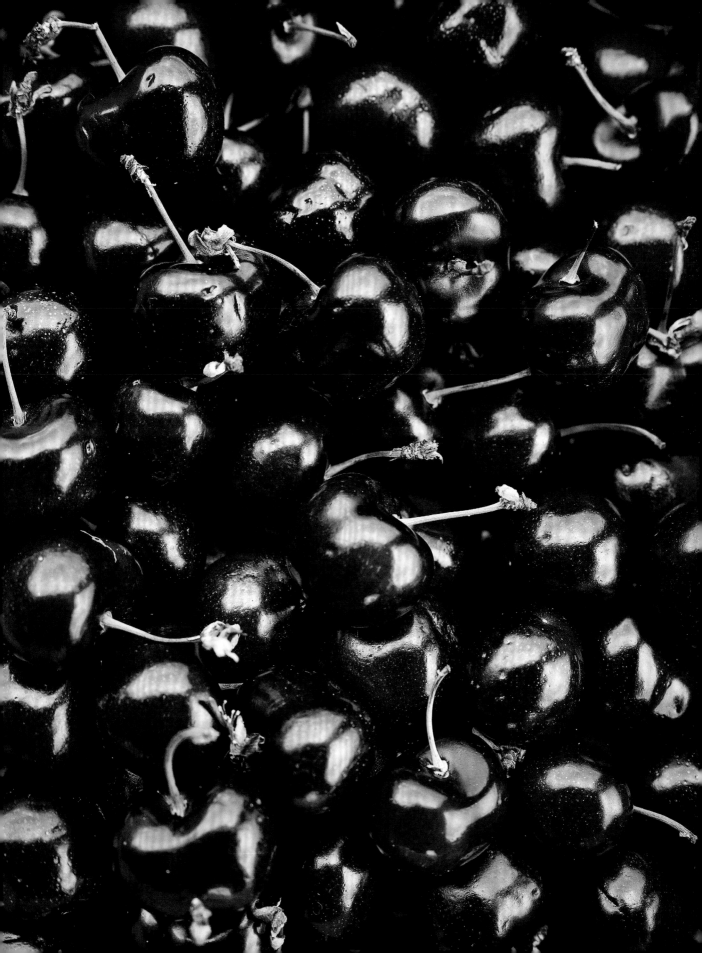

# TOLEDO TART BRIOCHE WITH POACHED PEARS AND HONEY

**Serves 8**

1 egg

125ml full-fat milk

250g white bread flour, plus extra
for dusting

25g caster sugar

5g salt

7g dried instant yeast

25g salted butter

200g marzipan, rolled into 8 balls

### For the pears

8 pears, peeled

rind and juice of 1 lemon

rind and juice of 1 orange

200g caster sugar

2 cinnamon sticks

**These delightful brioche tarts are filled with marzipan and then each topped with a citrus-poached pear. Toledo is a major producer of marzipan and you can find marzipan-flavoured sweets, cakes and nibbles all over the city. Marzipan from Toledo is also PGI (protected geographical indication) certified.**

To poach the pears, place them in a pan with the lemon and orange rind and juice, sugar, and cinnamon sticks, cover with water and bring to the boil. Reduce the heat and simmer for 20 minutes. Remove from the heat and leave to cool.

To make the brioche dough, put the egg and milk into the bowl of a stand mixer fitted with the dough hook attachment. Add the flour, sugar, salt and yeast and mix together, then add the butter. When the dough comes together, knead on a medium speed for 6–8 minutes. If you don't have a mixer, you can mix the ingredients together by hand, then knead for 8–10 minutes. Cover the dough in a bowl and leave to rest at room temperature for 1 hour until doubled in size.

Preheat the oven to 180°C (160°C fan)/350°F/gas 4.

Grease and line a baking tray with baking paper. On a lightly floured surface, roll the dough into eight circles, then place onto the prepared tray. Sit a marzipan ball on top of each dough circle, then a poached pear in the middle. Bake for 15 minutes until golden and baked through.

Bring the pear poaching liquor to the boil and reduce to a thick glaze. Brush all over the tarts and serve warm.

# BURNT BASQUE CHEESECAKE

**Serves 8**

---

butter, for greasing
800g cream cheese
200g sour cream
225g caster sugar
3 tablespoons plain flour
4 eggs
2 teaspoons vanilla extract
600g strawberries, hulled, to serve

**Everywhere in the Basque country you will see this dessert. Originating in San Sebastián and also known as torta de queso, this pudding combines a light and creamy texture with a deeply caramelised exterior. A true classic.**

Preheat the oven to 240°C (220°C fan)/475°F/gas 9.

Grease a 20cm deep springform tin and line it with baking paper. Whisk together the cream cheese, sour cream and sugar for 2 minutes, then add the flour, eggs and vanilla and whisk until smooth.

Pour into the prepared tin and bake for 20 minutes. Reduce the oven temperature to 180°C (160°C fan)/350°F/gas 4 and cook for another 20 minutes. Remove from the oven and leave to cool.

Chop the strawberries quite finely, then tip into a bowl. Serve with the cheesecake.

# WALNUT AND ORANGE CAKE

**Serves 6–8**

---

250g salted butter, plus extra
    for greasing
1 orange, zested and then sliced
1 tablespoon walnut liqueur
250g caster sugar
5 eggs
250g plain flour
1 teaspoon baking powder
100g walnuts, chopped

**For the glaze**
200g caster sugar
zest and juice of 1 orange
50ml walnut liqueur

**This simple one-layer sponge cake is my version of Spanish orange cake, which hails from Valencia. To change things up, I've flavoured my sponge not just with orange but also walnuts and added an extra layer of flavour with an orange juice and walnut liqueur glaze.**

Preheat the oven to 180°C (160°C fan)/350°F/gas 4. Grease and line a 20cm round cake tin with baking paper.

To make the cake, beat the butter, orange zest, walnut liqueur and sugar together in a stand mixer until fluffy. Add the eggs and beat until thoroughly mixed. Fold in the flour, baking powder and walnuts by hand.

Spoon into the prepared tin, top with the orange slices and bake on the middle shelf for 45 minutes.

Heat all the ingredients for the glaze together in a saucepan over a high heat for 5–6 minutes until syrupy. When the cake is nearly cold, brush the syrup all over the cake.

Serve slices of cake with cream or vanilla ice cream. It will keep in an airtight tin for 2–3 days.

# INDEX

# ACKNOWLEDGEMENTS

I would like to thank the team at ITV for letting me get to the milestone of 100 adventures in total and I'm so happy you like it. To all the people in Spain, suppliers, contributors and Porsche for making it all happen. The food team, Sam and Thatch, for getting this turned round and onto paper in record time. That goes for all the team at Quadrille too – it's been a pleasure yet again to work with you on this book. And above all, thank you all for watching over all these years. For all your support and continued loyalty, I thank you from myself and all the team.

James

**Cook's notes:**
All references to chorizo are for cooking chorizo. Tomato pulp can be made by finely chopping tomatoes or grating them using a box grater.

**Managing director:** Sarah Lavelle
**Project editor:** Vicky Orchard
**Designers:** Claire Rochford & Emily Lapworth
**Photography:** Dan Jones
**Head home economist:** Sam Head
**Home economist:** Alan Thatcher
**Home economist assistant:** George Head
**Props stylist:** Faye Wears
**Head of production:** Stephen Lang
**Senior production controller:** Katie Jarvis

First published in 2023 by Quadrille Publishing, an imprint of Hardie Grant Publishing

Quadrille, 52–54 Southwark Street, London SE1 1UN
www.quadrille.com

Text © 2023 James Martin
Photography © 2023 Dan Jones
Design and layout © 2023 Quadrille Publishing

Cataloguing in Publication Data: a catalogue record for this book is available from the British Library.

ISBN: 978 183783 129 6

Reprinted in 2023
10 9 8 7 6 5 4 3 2

Printed in Italy